LEARN TO DRAW WITH
PENCILS
PENS AND PASTELS

with 25 step-by-step drawing projects

IAN SIDAWAY AND SARAH HOGGETT

HERMES
HOUSE

This edition is published by Hermes House
an imprint of Anness Publishing Ltd
Hermes House, 88–89 Blackfriars Road, London SE1 8HA
tel. 020 7401 2077; fax 020 7633 9499
www.hermeshouse.com; www.annesspublishing.com

If you like the images in this book and would like to investigate using them for publishing, promotions or advertising, please visit our website www.practicalpictures.com for more information.
© Anness Publishing Ltd 2007, 2010

ETHICAL TRADING POLICY
At Anness Publishing we believe that business should be conducted in an ethical and ecologically sustainable way, with respect for the environment and a proper regard to the replacement of the natural resources we employ.
As a publisher, we use a lot of wood pulp in high-quality paper for printing, and that wood commonly comes from spruce trees. We are therefore currently growing more than 750,000 trees in three Scottish forest plantations: Berrymoss (130 hectares/320 acres), West Touxhill (125 hectares/305 acres) and Deveron Forest (75 hectares/185 acres). The forests we manage contain more than 3.5 times the number of trees employed each year in making paper for the books we manufacture. Because of this ongoing ecological investment programme, you, as our customer, can have the pleasure and reassurance of knowing that a tree is being cultivated on your behalf to naturally replace the materials used to make the book you are holding.Our forestry programme is run in accordance with the UK Woodland Assurance Scheme (UKWAS) and will be certified by the internationally recognized Forest Stewardship Council (FSC). The FSC is a non-government organization dedicated to promoting responsible management of the world's forests. Certification ensures forests are managed in an environmentally sustainable and socially responsible way. For further information about this scheme, go to www.annesspublishing.com/trees

Publisher: Joanna Lorenz
Editorial Director: Helen Sudell
Editors: James Harrison, Sarah Hoggett and Elizabeth Woodland
Photographer: George Taylor
Designer: Nigel Partridge
Cover designer: Nigel Partridge
Project contributors: Diana Constance; Abigail Edgar; Suzy Herbert; Wendy Jelbert; Melvyn Petterson; Paul Robinson; Ian Sidaway; Effie Waverlin
Editorial Reader: Rosie Fairhead
Production Controller: Lee Sargent
Previously published as part of a larger volume,
The Practical Encyclopedia of Drawing

Acknowledgements
Special thanks to the following artists for step-by-step demonstrations:
Diana Constance: pages 52–7, 64–7, 134–7, 138–43, 148–51.
Abigail Edgar: pages 8–9, 20–3, 30–1, 34–9, 60–1, 80–3, 86–7, 90–3, 98–101, 102–5, 108–9, 130–1, 138–43, 152–7.
Suzy Herbert: pages 68–71, 76–9, 116–19.
Wendy Jelbert: pages 6–7, 12–15, 16–19, 28–9, 44–7, 58–9, 84–5, 106–7, 120–3, 124–7, 128–9, 144–7.
Melvyn Petterson: pages 10–11; 24–7, 32–3, 40–3, 48–51, 62–3, 72–5, 88–9, 110–11, 112–15.
Paul Robinson: pages 94–7.
Thanks to the following for permission to reproduce copyright photographs:
Phil Dean: page 52(left). Jon Hibberd: pages 24 (bottom left), 98 (top), 108 (top), 112 (top), 116 (bottom left), 124 (top), 138. Anthony Pickhaver: page 144 (right). Megan Fishpool: page 62 (top). Keith at Imageworks: page 152 (top) with thanks to Valerie and Ben Lorenz for modelling. Also thanks to Francesco Mangiacasale for modelling.

PUBLISHER'S NOTE
Although the advice and information in this book are believed to be accurate and true at the time of going to press, neither the authors nor the publisher can accept any legal responsibility or liability for any errors or omissions that may have been made nor for any inaccuracies nor for any loss, harm or injury that comes about from following instructions or advice in this book.

Contents

Introduction

It is not easy to define the word 'drawing' because it embraces a wide range of different activities. At its simplest it can be described as marks made on a sheet of paper, and in this sense it is one of the most basic of human activities.

Drawing is often regarded as a special gift, and it is true that there are people who seem to be able to draw quite effortlessly. Yet drawing, like writing, is a skill which can be acquired; if the motivation is there, most people can learn to draw accurately.

The word 'drawing' no longer conjures up an image of timid grey pencil marks on white paper – much more exciting effects than this are achievable. It can be a few lines in a sketchbook, made to remind the artist of some salient point in a subject, the first step in painting, or a finished work of art in its own right, planned, and executed with as much thought as a painting.

Cityscape ▼
For this drawing of a construction site, the artist has used oil pastel, an ideal medium for bold effects and quick impressions as colours can be built up rapidly.

There is now a wider choice of drawing materials than ever before. In fact a selection of pencils – a 2H, HB, 2B, 4B and 6B should be adequate for most purposes – charcoal, coloured pencils, pastels, inks and a pad of paper are more than enough for most people's needs to begin with. As you practise and develop your own style, you will build up a collection of equipment as you go along.

Once you have bought your basic equipment, the next step is to become thoroughly familiar with the materials that you are using and to learn how they behave. In this book there are 45 specially commissioned projects that cover all the popular subjects: portraits and figures, still lifes and animals, landscapes and buildings, and trees and flowers. You will find that each project is easy to follow with detailed colour photographs illustrating each step.

Do not worry if your first attempts do not look exactly like the ones reproduced here. The most scary thing for every artist is simply getting over initial inhibitions about making the first marks on a blank sheet of paper. Set aside a little time for drawing each day, if you can – and after a couple of weeks, look back and assess your progress. You will be amazed at how far you have come.

The subject matter is limitless, from a simple but dramatic study of trees in winter to a detailed drawing of a short-eared owl, from an elegant study of a Venetian building on a white background to a portrait of a much-loved family pet, you will find something here to suit all tastes.

Practise these projects over the course of an afternoon – or you may even decide to spread them out over several sessions. You can either copy the projects step by step, exactly as shown here, or use them as a starting point for your own artistic explorations. All the projects are packed with useful tips and general principles that you can apply to subjects of your own choosing – so take the time to study them carefully, even if you do not reproduce them all.

You will find many different approaches here – some finely detailed, some with careful build-ups of tone and colour; others much looser and more impressionistic. All approaches are valid and you will almost certainly have your own preferences. The most important thing is to realize just how much you can learn from looking at other artists' work. There are also quick sketches covering a wide range of the most popular subjects. These works will provide you with inspiration, ideas and practical information on how to approach each of these themes.

All the artists featured in this book have built up a wealth of experience over many years of study, which they share here with you in the hope that you will gain as much pleasure and enjoyment from drawing with pen and ink, pencils and pastels as they have experienced. With time and a bit of practice, you will soon be creating works of art that you will feel proud to display to friends and family.

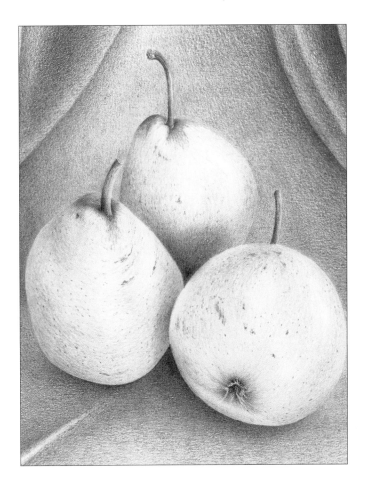

Still life with pears ▲
Layers of coloured pencils have been built up to achieve meticulous detail and depth of colour using a delicate shading technique so that almost no lines are visible.

Quick sketches of people: At the beach ▶
Pen and ink can achieve intricate and elaborate effects. It is also a good medium for rapid location drawings like this as the impossibility of erasing encourages a decisive approach.

Quick sketches of trees: Damaged tree

Trees are a delight to draw – particularly old trees that have gnarled bark and twists and splits in their trunks – as they allow you to explore a wide range of textural techniques and approaches to making marks. Monochrome sketches are perhaps the most interesting and satisfying of all as, without the distraction of colour, the textures and shapes really start to come into their own.

It's important to try to convey a sense of trees as living, growing organisms, and you should always examine the shapes of the trunk and branches carefully before you start to draw: some trees, such as the silver birch, have thin, relatively smooth trunks, while others, such as ancient olives that have been cultivated for many decades, have gnarled trunks with distinct grooved patterns in the surface. If you're sketching *in situ*, try running your fingers over the trunk to get a feel for the texture and the pattern of the bark: does the pattern run up and down in fairly straight lines or does it go round in nobbly circles?

Look at how the branches grow out of the main trunk: do they spread out straight, or veer upwards in a v-shaped pattern on either side of the trunk, or droop downwards? Finally, think about how you're going to draw the leaves. For small leaves, a few loose dots and dashes may be sufficient; for larger leaves you may need to be more precise about the shape – but don't overdo the leaf detailing, or you'll detract from the shape of the tree as a whole.

The scene
This tree was badly damaged in a winter gale. The artist came across it when she was out for a walk in the country and was attracted by the shapes made by the broken and contorted branches and by the gnarled texture of the bark.

5-minute sketch: graphite pencil
After putting down the outline with slightly jagged pencil strokes, the artist then scribbled in the darkest areas of tone, such as the undersides of the branches and the shaded interior of the split in the trunk. Even in a quick five-minute sketch such as this, you can begin to capture something of the form of the tree.

10-minute sketch: graphite pencil
In a slightly longer sketch, you can begin to refine the detail, putting in tones that range from a mid-grey on the shaded parts to a much denser black in the hollowed recess near the base. In addition to providing information about the light and shade, the tone is applied in such as way as to hint at the pattern of the bark.

15-minute sketch: graphite pencil

The shading is more highly developed in this sketch and the tree looks more three-dimensional. Although the background is not drawn in detail, putting in the horizon and blocking in generalized shapes for the trees and bushes in the distance sets the tree in context.

25-minute sketch: graphite pencil plus pen and ink

Confident, scribbled pen lines over an initial pencil sketch give this drawing a real sense of energy and capture the character of the tree very well. Note the use of a wide range of marks, from simple hatching on the trunk to tiny flecks and dashes for the small leaves.

Quick sketches of trees: Foliage masses

Trees form an important part of many landscapes and can also be used as a compositional device, to lead the viewer's eye into the scene or to provide a natural 'frame'. Different types of foliage, however, require different artistic approaches. One of the most common mistakes is to attempt to put in too much detail. Start by looking at the shape of the tree: is it conical or rounded? Then look at the shapes of the leaves within the foliage mass: are they large with a distinctive shape, such as a maple or horse chestnut, or are there many small leaves clustered tightly together, as in the example on these pages? Finally, look for the differences in tone that will make the foliage masses look three-dimensional. Even in dull lighting, as here, some areas will be lighter than others; half closing your eyes as you look at the scene will make it much easier to assess this.

The scene
The dark mass of the tree on the left forms a natural 'frame' for the mountainous, wooded landscape beyond and helps to give a sense of scale. The artist elected to make a number of studies of this single tree in order to capture its character.

5-minute sketch: charcoal
Start by loosely blocking in the overall shape using the side of the charcoal stick, then work into this shape with the tip of the charcoal, scribbling and dotting in the darkest parts of the foliage mass to create some variation in tone so that the tree begins to look three-dimensional. Smooth out the charcoal with your fingertip or a torchon.

15-minute sketch: 4B pencil, black ballpoint pen
Graphite pencils and ballpoint pens are perfect for reference sketches on location as they are easily portable and not messy. The artist roughly blocked in the shape with a 4B pencil, which makes a lovely, dense mark, before hatching in the darkest areas with a black ballpoint pen. The closer together the hatched lines, the darker and denser the tone will be.

30-minute sketch: coloured wax pencils

With wax pencils you can quickly build up areas of broken colour and create lively optical mixes that capture the full range of tones within the foliage mass. Start with the lightest colour first – a pale, yellowy green. Then add progressively darker greens until you achieve the effect that you want, using a carefully controlled scribble. Some areas are very dark indeed, but beware of using a solid black as it can 'deaden' the overall effect; instead, use dark, reddish browns that complement the greens and give some warmth to the scene. (Look closely at any subject and you will often see that the shadow areas contain a dark colour that is complementary to the colour of the main subject.)

Quick sketches of flowers: Poppies

Some flowers, such as bedding plants in a municipal park, grow in straight, regimented lines. Others grow in untrammelled profusion, their stems twisting and turning over one another, the flower heads flopping in all directions. When you draw or paint flowers, allow the natural growth pattern to dictate your artistic approach so that you can capture the essential character of the plant.

These poppies seem to rise and pop up almost at random. Artistically, the rich colours and ruffled shapes call for a free, impressionistic approach. The translucent petals provide plenty of opportunity to explore tonal contrasts and colour mixes, as deeper tones are created where petals overlap or cast shadows on neighbouring petals. Powdery media such as charcoal and soft pastel are perfect for this subject. The black centres and seed heads offer interesting contrasts of colour and shape; here, you can make stronger, linear marks.

5-minute sketch: black and white soft pastels

If you only have five minutes or so to spare, you will not have time to sketch more than one or two individual blooms. Nonetheless, this is a good loosening-up and observational exercise. Here, loose, light white pastel lines recreate the frilly edges of the poppy petals, with more controlled marks being made for the seed heads. Finally, the artist has scribbled in black pastel for the very dark flower centres.

The scene
The artist came across this patch of poppies growing in a corner of her garden and wanted to create the feeling of random, spontaneous growth. Deliberately cutting off the edges of some of the poppies in her sketches helps to convey this: such a subject should not appear too neat and tidy!

10-minute sketch: charcoal
In a very quick sketch like this one, you need to concentrate first on capturing the shapes of the flowers and the individual petals within them. At the same time, try to keep your marks loose and spontaneous. Don't worry if the shapes are not completely perfect because the main aim is to get the general feeling right. Here, the artist used free-flowing, calligraphic marks to delineate the shapes of the petals, smudging the charcoal to create the darkest tones on the flowers.

15-minute sketch: inks, dip pen and brush, and rollerball pen

Pen and ink is a good medium for sketching the spiky texture of the poppy leaves – but again, in order to create a feeling of spontaneity, you should try to keep your pen marks fairly loose and jagged. The artist first sketched the outlines with the dip pen. Then she brushed varying dilutions of coloured inks over the top, to create the petals, with the darker tones being used where the translucent petals overlap one another. She used a rollerball pen for details such as the stamens, as it gives a less crude line than the dip pen. Note how effective it is to leave much of the image uncoloured. Blocking in every single petal could easily have produced a rather tight and laboured image that failed to capture the character of the flowers.

30-minute sketch: soft pastels

Soft pastels are a lovely medium for the translucent petals, as you can blend the colours to create lively optical mixes and subtle transitions in tone. At the same time, you need to make sure that the edges of the petals are clearly delineated, which you can do using the tip of a slightly lighter-coloured pastel. The artist used a cool blue pastel paper because this is an appropriate colour for the background and allows the flowers themselves – which are much warmer in tone – to come forwards in the image. Flowing, calligraphic marks capture the character of the flowers in a similar vein to the other quick sketches on these pages.

Trees in winter

Monochrome media such as charcoal or graphite are perfect for wintry scenes; there is relatively little colour so you can concentrate on tone and texture. With the coming of winter the underlying shape of deciduous trees, which is largely disguised by leaves in other seasons of the year, becomes apparent. In some species such as willow, the main boughs droop down; chestnut trees spread in a gentle arc, while some pine trees are basically conical in shape. It's a good idea to look for the overall geometric shapes first and sketch them in very lightly before you add any detail.

One of the most important things to remember when drawing trees is that the branches are not mere appendages, stuck on as an afterthought in the way they might be in a young child's drawing, but an organic part of the tree as a whole. Look at each tree in its entirety, instead of drawing the trunk first and adding the branches later. Look at the negative shapes – the spaces in between – as well as at the positive shapes of the branches.

Branches are such solid, heavy things that it may strike you as odd to draw them in outline and leave them as white shapes, as the artist does here. Look closely at this scene, however, and you will see that they are actually lighter in tone than the mass of ivy leaves behind. If you were to block them in with a mid-tone of grey, they would not stand out clearly. In areas where they are silhouetted against the bland white sky, you can use dark pencil marks.

Materials
- *Smooth drawing paper*
- *6B pencil*

The scene
A group of trees is starkly silhouetted against the white sky and the snow-covered ground, with just a few exposed patches of earth adding texture to the foreground. The trees are very near the centre of the image, which is generally not considered advisable, but in this case, the central placement is one way of conveying the calm, still mood of the scene.

1 Using a 6B pencil, which makes a strong, dense mark, put in the main lines of the trees. Remember to look at the negative shapes – the spaces between the branches – as well as at the branches themselves. Also indicate the fence posts and a few small bushes in the middle distance, remembering to make the posts smaller as they recede.

2 Loosely block in the main areas of ivy so that you begin to establish the structure of the trees. Don't try to put in individual leaves or any texture at this stage – this will come later. Remember to leave spaces where the branches lie over the top of the ivy and keep checking to make sure you're not covering any major branches that need to be left white.

3 Continue working on the negative spaces between the branches of the trees until you have blocked in all the clumps of ivy.

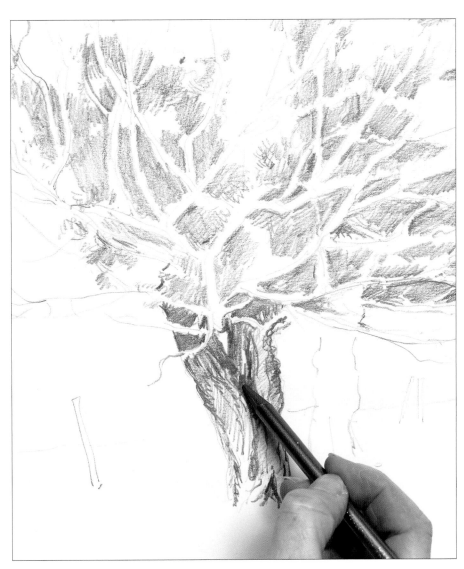

4 Now shade in the trunks, making short, jagged pencil marks with the tip of the pencil to convey the texture of the bark. Note that the trunk of the foremost tree is split; darken one side of the split to make it clear that one part of the tree stands in front of the other part. Even though there is no textural detail in the foliage, and the branches have simply been left as white shapes, the trees are already beginning to take shape.

5 Block in the trunk of the second tree in the same way and dot in fallen leaves and exposed clumps of earth in the foreground. As you work, pay careful attention to where the main branches jut forwards in front of the trunk; allow them to remain white so that their position in relation to the dark trunk behind is clear.

6 Now that the clumps of ivy have been blocked in, you can begin to put in more texture, by adding loose scribbles over the main blocks and dotting in some of the smaller clumps and individual leaves towards the extremities of the branches. Don't be too precise about the placing of the leaves – try to create a general impression of the way the ivy grows.

▶

7 At the extremities, reinforce the lines of the branches in front of or parallel to the trunks with strong pencil marks, applying more pressure than you have done so far. There are lots of kinks and twists in the branches; make sure you convey this in your line work. Leave the largest branches in front of the trunks as white negative shapes so that they stand out against the darkness of the bark and the ivy.

Assessment time

The trees are taking shape well and the differences in tone help us to see where one trunk or branch is positioned in relation to others, with the darker elements appearing to advance towards us while lighter ones appear to be farther away. However, at this stage the trees seem almost to be floating in a void; you need to anchor them within the landscape by adding more detail to the fence posts and the bushes in the middle distance.

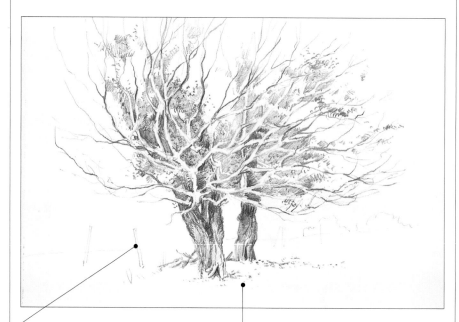

Strengthening the fence posts will make the setting clearer and help to lead the viewer's eye through the picture.

Adding more texture to the ground in front of the trees will help to set them in the context of the landscape.

8 Because the bushes in the middle distance are further away than the trees, they appear to be lighter in tone. Block them in, applying medium pressure to the pencil so that you create a mid-tone rather than the very dense, solid greys and blacks used for the trees.

9 Block in the fence posts, making the two posts on the left of the image very dark and the others less so, so that you create a feeling of recession. Put some light shading in the foreground; even though it is covered in snow, the shadows reveal the undulations in the ground.

The finished drawing

Against the white sky, the starkness of the trees makes for a bold, graphic image. With flowing, confident pencil lines, the artist has created an image in which the branches grow organically out of the tree trunks, twisting and turning over one another. There is just enough detail around the trees, in the form of the fence posts, a few small bushes, and some textural detail in the immediate foreground, to hint at the landscape in which they are situated.

Confident, flowing lines capture the trees' growth pattern beautifully.

Jagged pencil marks convey the texture of the bark.

Soft mid-tones in the middle distance help to create a sense of recession.

Field of sunflowers

A field of bright yellow sunflowers in full bloom is a dazzling sight and one that has attracted many artists and photographers. But although the colour is the first thing that attracts your eye, it isn't necessarily enough to make a successful drawing: you also need to make sure that there's a focal point to the image, so spend plenty of time choosing the right viewpoint. Select a place where some flowers are face on and others are partially turned away, as this allows you to examine the structure of the flowers and introduce some variety into the way that you draw them. Also make sure that the flower heads are at different heights, so that you don't get a straight line running across the image.

The background is important, too – both the fields in the distance and the spaces between the plants. Although it's relatively indistinct in this scene, it sets the sunflowers within the context of the landscape. Half-close your eyes to assess which tones and colours to use – and don't be too literal in your rendition. Aim, instead, to create lively mixes of colour on the support by applying several layers of thin colour. Also make sure that the background hangs together as a whole and that no one part jumps forwards too much in the scene.

This is a complicated scene, with lots of different elements. To prevent yourself from getting bogged down in too much detail, concentrate on the negative shapes between the flowers. It's often easier to see these shapes than it is to draw the positive shapes (the flowers themselves).

Materials
- *Good-quality drawing paper*
- *Coloured pencils: a selection of pale, mid-toned and dark blues and greens, burnt sienna, canary yellow, lemon yellow, yellow ochre, light brown and lilac*

The scene
Although this scene might look a little confusing on first glance, the artist selected her viewpoint carefully to ensure that the sunflower heads made interesting shapes and were positioned at different heights within the picture area.

1 When you've chosen your viewpoint, lightly sketch the scene using burnt sienna for the sunflowers and pale blues for the shapes of the fields in the background. Look at the spaces between the flowers, and at where they overlap one another, as well as at the individual flower heads.

2 Loosely colour in the background fields with a range of blues and greens, with touches of burnt sienna in places for the exposed patches of earth, getting slightly darker as you move towards the foreground. As you reach the sunflower field, begin to fill in the negative shapes between the stems.

3 Start blocking in the yellow petals of the largest sunflowers using a canary yellow pencil for the darker yellows and lemon yellow for the brighter yellows.

4 Continue blocking in the yellows, varying the tones as appropriate. Block in the negative shapes in the immediate foreground in blue, using loose scribbles.

5 Continue the process of blocking in the negative spaces between the sunflowers that you began in Step 2, using a range of blues and greens as appropriate. Note that the colour is not uniform: look for differences between the warm and the cool tones, as some areas are cast into shadow by the sunflower leaves and flowers while others are in bright sunlight.

6 Work over the background fields again, gradually darkening them. Colour in the flower centres. Note that some are darker than others: alternate between yellow ochre and burnt sienna.

▶

Assessment time

Achieving the correct tonal values is a gradual process and one that cannot be rushed, but now that all the elements are in place you should take the time to stand back and look at the drawing as a whole to assess how much more needs to be done. You can see that the drawing is too pale overall and that more contrast between the lightest and darkest areas is required. In addition, more modelling is required on the main subject – the sunflowers.

7 Using dark blue block in the bluer tones of the background fields with vertical scribbles, getting darker as you come towards the foreground.

The sunflowers look rather flat and somewhat two-dimensional.

The leaves do not stand out clearly against the background.

8 Apply brown over some of the brighter background greens to soften them. Block in some of the brown stalks. Some flowers are partially turned away from the sun: apply brown pencil over these areas.

9 Loosely scribble blue over the sky. Work on the background, trying to develop some texture and a range of shapes and tones. Work on the negative spaces between the flowers again, delineating the edges with dark greens and blues, and darken the yellows of the sunflowers.

10 Adjust the colours and shading across the image as a whole, applying touches of warmer colours such as lilac in the foreground to make this area seem closer to the viewer. Using the tip of the pencil, apply some veining to the leaves in the immediate foreground.

The finished drawing

With the flower heads and leaves turning and twisting at different angles, this drawing is full of interest. There is just enough of the landscape in the background to convey something of the setting, while the spaces between the plants in the foreground provide a darker backdrop against which the leaves and flowers can stand out.

Simple shading makes the flowers look three-dimensional.

The leaves stand out well against the dark negative spaces between the plants.

The colour is paler on the distant fields, creating a convincing sense of recession.

Flower-filled alleyway

Scenes of alleyways with whitewashed buildings adorned with brightly coloured plants are commonplace in Greece, Spain, Portugal and other Mediterranean countries and are the perfect reminder of an enjoyable holiday.

When drawing flowers you have to choose between a very detailed drawing which is botanically accurate in every respect, or a more impressionistic approach that captures the mood of the scene, as the artist does here. Oil pastels are an excellent medium for this approach. With their broad tips they are not suitable for precise linear details, but they can be used for bold spots of colour.

The key to this scene is to make sure there is enough contrast between the very dark and the very light areas. Here, the brightest areas are created by using the white of the support: as you can't make the light areas any lighter than this, the only way to ensure sufficient contrast is to make the darks really dark. At the same time, you need to maintain some textural detail in the areas of shadow.

Materials

- *Oil sketching paper*
- *Oil pastels: pale grey, turquoise blue, mid-brown, purplish blue, bright green, reddish brown, orange, grey-black, dark green, crimson, cadmium yellow deep, mid-green, black, white, olive green*
- *Turpentine or paint thinner and clean rag*

The scene

A wedge-shaped shadow on the left directs the viewer's eye towards the flowers scrambling up the wall on the right-hand side. The pale-coloured stonework acts as a foil for the bright flowers and adds an interesting contrast of texture.

1 Using a pale grey oil pastel, sketch the main lines of the scene – the buildings, with their windows and doors, and the large wedge-shaped shadow that juts across the alley from the left. Measure the proportions and angles carefully; if you're unsure, put in the lines lightly in pencil first, as pencil is much easier to erase than oil pastel.

2 Using a turquoise blue oil pastel, block in the sky. Block in the shadow with a mid-brown oil pastel and go over it with purplish blue and turquoise. (Shadows are never a single, uniform colour.) Using the purplish blue and turquoise pastels, block in the shadows cast on the right-hand wall by the flowers.

3 Using the side of a pale grey pastel, loosely block in the sides of the buildings that are in shadow and the long, thin shadows that run across the foreground. Don't press heavily on the pastel or the coverage will be too thick, making it difficult to apply subsequent layers and achieve lively, interesting colour mixes in the shadows.

4 Dip a rag in turpentine or in white spirit and rub the rag gently over the sky and shadows to blend the pastel marks to a smooth colour.

> ■ **Tip**: Use a clean section of rag for each area that you blend, so as not to muddy the colours.

5 Using a bright green oil pastel, loosely scribble in the lightest green of the foliage and the iron gates at the end of the alleyway. Don't make your marks too specific, as you will refine the shapes and colours later; these loose strokes give the impression of uncontrolled growth. Use a reddish brown pastel to block in the shape of the large terracotta pot on the wall.

6 Using a reddish brown oil pastel, put in the door and woodwork. Soften the colour in places by adding a little orange over the top, blending the colours on the support by rubbing them together. Add grey-black for the tiled roof between the buildings. Scribble in very dark green throughout the scene for the darkest foliage. The image is now beginning to take on some depth.

7 Block in the red flowers in crimson and the lighter flowers in cadmium yellow deep. Both are warm colours, so the flowers immediately jump forwards in the scene. Scribble in the mid-tones of the foliage using a bright mid-green. The range of foliage tones helps to give the image depth as the light and dark tones hint at shadow areas within the leaves. Although the leaves are not drawn in detail, the use of different colours shows that there are several types of foliage in the scene.

8 The large shadow on the left is an important part of the composition, but now that the rest of the picture is beginning to take on some form, it appears too pale and flat. Add a little blue, green and purple to this area and blend the colours with a rag soaked in turpentine or white spirit. Keep the coverage patchy, however, to help create the texture of the ground. Draw the cracks in the paving in black oil pastel, making strong linear marks of varying degrees of intensity.

9 Block in the metal gate in the background in mid-green and use fine vertical lines of dark green for the individual bars. Draw the flowers on the background building, dotting in the general shapes and moving between light and dark tones to create a sense of form. Lightly apply pale grey over the shaded side of the background building. Indicate some of the horizontal courses in the stonework using grey and orange overlaid with white for a pinky terracotta colour.

10 Using the tip of the pastel and making jagged, spiky marks that jut out from the main stems, apply strokes of dark olive green to the stems in the foreground.

Tip: These spiky, linear marks create more detail and texture in the immediate foreground, which is one way to create a sense of depth in a drawing.

Assessment time

Now that the drawing is very nearly complete, you should take some time to assess the overall balance. Ask yourself, for example, if there is enough contrast between the very bright sunlit patches on the ground and the very dense shadows. Is there enough detail in the flowers and stems in the immediate foreground? Even very small adjustments at this stage can make a difference.

The shadow has been skilfully rendered but the area would benefit from a little more textural detail.

11 Even within an area that appears, at first glance, to be very dark, some texture should be evident. Where necessary, add a few small linear marks using a black pastel – but take care not to overdo it.

12 Working lightly and quickly, add very thin vertical strokes of white, grey and yellow to the grasses in the immediate foreground to create more depth and enhance the spiky texture.

The finished drawing

There is a lovely sense of light and shade, and of warm and cool areas, in this drawing. Note how the artist has left some areas of the paper almost untouched, so that the white of the support is allowed to stand for the dazzling patches of sunlight. Bold dashes of colour for the flowers and leaves combine with smoothly blended passages such as the sky and the large foreground shadow, creating a generalized impression of the scene, rather than a detailed rendition in which every flower or crack in the wall can be seen. The overall effect is very lively and appealing – the perfect reminder of a holiday in a sunny clime.

Although we cannot see the building on the left, its presence is implied by the very strong shadow, which also serves to lead the viewer's eye into the scene.

The smoothness of the sky (created by blending the pastel marks with a rag dipped in a solvent) contrasts well with the texture of the buildings and plants.

Although the individual leaf and flower shapes are not drawn precisely, the use of a range of tones creates a convincing three-dimensional feel.

Autumn leaf

From delicate yellowy-golds through to rich russets and reds, autumn leaves contain a wonderful range of colours. Even a single leaf can make a very attractive study. If you're new to working in soft pastels, this is the ideal project to start with. As the colours merge together in a random way, you can practise blending colours without having to worry too much about exactly where you place each one.

Use some artistic licence when it comes to drawing the background. You can choose between lightly sketching some generalized leaf shapes or laying down an overall colour, rather like out-of-focus leaf litter. Whatever you decide, try to get some variety and interesting blends into this area as a flat application of a single colour can look very bland and boring.

Pastel papers come in a wide range of colours. Here, the artist has used a pale peach-coloured pastel paper, which is much more sympathetic to the glowing autumn leaf than stark white paper.

Materials
- *Pale peach pastel paper*
- *Soft pastels: pale cadmium yellow, lemon yellow, cadmium yellow, light red, burnt sienna, burnt umber, cadmium orange, white, yellow ochre, ultramarine blue*

The leaf
It is the lighting that makes this leaf so interesting: it allows the veins on the leaf to stand out prominently. Note how the stem is on the diagonal, which makes the image more dynamic than if it were straight.

1 Draw the outline of the leaf and its stem in pale cadmium yellow pastel, putting in the central vein as a guide to help you judge where things are. Using a lemon yellow pastel, loosely scribble over the whole leaf. Although this will be modified by subsequent colours, it establishes the overall base colour.

2 Make the lemon yellow pastel coverage looser in the centre. Scribble cadmium yellow (be aware this is poisonous) around the edges and blend with your fingers so that the individual pastel strokes cannot be seen.

> **Tip**: Use the tip of your finger and work inwards, towards the centre of the leaf, so that you don't push pastel on to the background.

3 Stroke light red over the top of the leaf, where the reddest tones occur, and blend with your fingers. Touch burnt sienna into the darkest areas at the top of the leaf and blend. Draw the veins in burnt sienna.

4 Continue using burnt sienna at the top of the leaf, blending the marks with your fingers as you go. Reinforce the veins with burnt umber. Blend cadmium orange over the top of the leaf and around the veins.

5 Now that the main colours are in place, you can start to add some detail. Using the tip of the pastel, carefully draw along the veins in white to begin to highlight the leaf's delicate framework.

6 Apply pale yellow over the lightest parts of the leaf and the main veins. Blend small spots of lemon yellow over the lower half of the leaf so that it starts to take on a rich, warm glow. Using the tip of the pastel, draw along the shaded sides of the veins in burnt umber. Note how the veins are beginning to stand out from the rest of the leaf.

Assessment time
Draw around the edge of the leaf in burnt umber to define it.
This helps to make the shape clearer, but the leaf still looks a little flat and two-dimensional. You need to build up the form and put in some kind of background so that the leaf really comes forward in the scene.

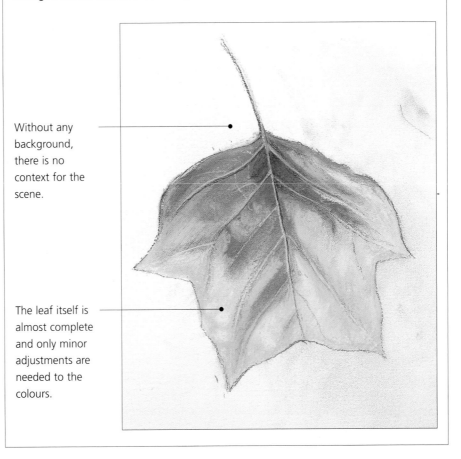

Without any background, there is no context for the scene.

The leaf itself is almost complete and only minor adjustments are needed to the colours.

7 Start to put in the background by roughly sketching the shape of other leaves behind. Draw around the top right of the leaf in burnt umber to imply the bark of the tree behind. Scribble yellows, oranges and reds over the background, making the colours next to the leaf quite dark so that it looks as if the leaf is casting a shadow on those behind.

8 Your scribbles have helped to bring the leaf forwards in the scene. Now apply more colour to the background to imply that there are leaves in this area, too – yellow ochre, a little burnt umber, and any other colours in the same colour range. Blend the colours lightly with your fingers, so that the coverage is fairly smooth but some textural marks are still visible.

9 Continue blocking in the background with yellow ochre and other colours, and add a little ultramarine blue and burnt umber, so that the background is darker than the leaf. Blend the area with your fingertips.

10 Continue working on the background, using the same range of colours as before and blending the marks with your fingers, until you're satisfied with the colours and the overall balance.

The finished drawing

This is a relatively simple exercise, but it demonstrates the potential and versatility of soft pastels. The pastel marks have been smoothed out to create almost imperceptible transitions from one colour to another, and the leaf has a luminous glow that is characteristic of late-afternoon sunlight in autumn. The careful application of light and dark tones on the veins has made them look convincingly three-dimensional and these crisp, unblended lines add another texture to the study.

The pastel marks on the leaf have been blended on the support to create smooth areas of colour.

The crisp detail given to the leaf veins adds contrasting interest and a focus to the leaf structure.

Vague leaf shapes in the background suggest the natural woodland setting that lies beyond.

Quick sketches of landscapes: Riverbank

A riverside setting has lots of potential for interesting landscape sketches. If the river runs swiftly, there will be splashes and swirling eddies as the water breaks around rocks and other objects. Gentle ripples create a different mood, slightly distorting any reflections. Occasionally, you come across a hidden pool in which the water appears to be completely still, where the reflections are sharp and crisp. Each requires a different approach, from dynamic, energetic marks for rapidly flowing water to a more measured, controlled approach for very still water and reflections.

Whatever the mood of the river, it is often a good idea to use it as a compositional device to lead the viewer's eye through the picture. Bear this in mind when you position yourself on the bank to take a reference photo or make a sketch. A view along a river, so you can see how it meanders its way through the surrounding area, is almost always more satisfying in compositional terms than one looking straight across from one bank to the other as, in the latter case, the river will form a broad horizontal band that cuts the composition in two and blocks the viewer's eye from moving any further through the scene.

When you're drawing water, always remember that it takes its colour from surrounding objects – although the colour is generally slightly more muted in the reflection than it is in the object itself. In a riverside setting the greens and browns of nearby trees may be reflected in the water; alternatively, there may be patches of sky that are so bright that you need apply virtually no colour whatsoever.

The scene
Here, the river forms a gentle curve that leads our eye through the scene to the buildings on the horizon. The sky is very bright and bland, with no dramatic cloud formations to add interest to the scene, so the reflections of the trees along the bank provide a feature in what would otherwise be a completely empty area.

5-minute sketch: sepia water-soluble pencil
Five minutes is plenty of time for you to work out a composition for a larger drawing. Make a quick thumbnail sketch, roughly outlining the shapes of the main elements (including the reflections).

10-minute sketch: sepia water-soluble pencil
A tonal study will require a little more time. Here, the artist lightly brushed a little clean water over some of the pencil marks to blend them to a tonal wash, leaving the brightest areas untouched.

15-minute sketch: sepia water-soluble pencil

In this sketch, more textural detail is evident. It is created by using the water-soluble pencil dry (on the grass on the near bank, for example) and on slightly damp paper, so that the marks spread a little (on the large tree on the far bank).

30-minute sketch: sepia water-soluble pencil

In the longest sketch of the series, the scene is beginning to look more three-dimensional. Note how some elements, such as the large tree on the far bank and the grass in the foreground of the near bank, are given more textural marks, which helps to indicate that they are nearer the viewer and create a sense of recession in the scene.

Quick sketches of landscapes: Mountain track

When you're drawing or sketching on location, particularly when you're faced with a panoramic view, it's very easy to get carried away by the grandeur of the setting and lose sight of the fact that your image needs to work as a composition. Always look for something that you can use as a focal point, such as a large boulder or a tree, and place it at a strong point in the picture space so that the viewer's eye goes immediately to it. Look for lines (real or imaginary) that lead the viewer's eye

through the scene – maybe a wall or a fence, a line of bushes or, as here, a stony track leading into the distance.

To convey the scale of the scene and create a convincing sense of recession, you must also remember the rules of aerial and linear perspective: objects that are further away should appear smaller and paler in tone than those that are close by. Having more texture and detail in the foreground is another way of making this part of the image appear closer.

The scene
The track directs our attention to the mountains in the distance, while the rocks on the left provide a much-needed focal point.

5-minute sketch: charcoal
Compositionally, the track is an obvious way of drawing our attention to the backdrop, as are the wedge-shaped slopes on the left and right. Once she had worked out the composition, the artist scribbled down some very rough, linear marks for the pebbly track and rocks, and smudged charcoal to create broad areas of dark and mid-tone. The mountains were largely left untouched, so that they are paler than the foreground areas, which helps to create a feeling of recession.

15-minute sketch: chisel-tip pen

You may never have thought of using an ordinary fibre-tip pen as a drawing tool but, although it is not the most sophisticated of implements, it can be very useful for making quick sketches on location as it is easily portable and clean to handle. By adjusting the angle at which you hold it and by applying differing amounts of pressure, you will also find that it can make a surprisingly varied range of marks. Here, the artist used spiky vertical marks to convey the texture of the grasses, while rough circles describe the pebbles on the track and wispy curves imply the fluffy clouds overhead. The chisel-shaped tip of the pen was used to block in larger elements such as the trees, bushes and boulders, creating a convincing sense of solidity in these areas. Note how the amount of visible detail decreases with distance: apart from a few sketchy lines to indicate the contours, the distant mountains are left blank.

30-minute sketch: soft pastels

A cream pastel paper gives an underlying warmth to the image; the tooth of the paper also has an effect, as it helps to convey the texture of the pebble-strewn ground. Note how many different greens and yellows the artist has used. She has overlaid them to create lively colour mixes and blended them in parts so that areas of soft grass contrast effectively with the hard texture of the rocks.

Quick sketches of landscapes: Field of rape

Don't ignore the potential of man-made landscapes such as arable crops: they can provide you with subjects that are every bit as colourful and intriguing as wild, rugged scenes. Start by looking for something that you can use as the main centre of interest in your drawing – a lone tree, farm machinery rusting away in a corner, or a distant farmhouse, for example – and place it at a strong position in the picture space. If there is no obvious focal point, as in the images on these two pages, decide what it is that makes you want to draw the scene. Here, it is obviously the mass of brightly coloured flowers. In a situation such as this, where almost all the plants are the same height, select your viewpoint carefully and pay attention to the negative spaces in between the plants in order to create a well-balanced composition.

5-minute sketch: ballpoint pen

This is a compositional sketch: the converging lines of the hedgerow on the left and the line of trees in the background create strong, dark lines against which the lighter flowers will stand out clearly. The artist has indicated the darkest areas within the flowers by means of swiftly hatched lines, leaving the paper white for the densely packed mass of flowers in the bottom left of the image.

The scene

Meadows and fields of crops such as this rape in flower make colourful subjects for landscape drawings and paintings. Here, the artist selected a relatively low viewpoint, which gave a large mass of flowers in the bottom left of the image. The hedgerow on the left and the line of trees in the background jut up above the field, providing much-needed vertical elements in the composition. Their dark, straight lines also help to concentrate the viewer's attention on the flowers.

15-minute sketch: 4B graphite stick

This is a slightly more elaborate sketch than the one on the previous page: the artist had time to begin exploring the range of tones within the scene. Once he had established the dark, solid lines of the hedgerow and trees, he concentrated largely on the negative shapes – the dark spaces between the stems – scribbling them in with the tip of the graphite stick.

30-minute sketch: pastel pencils

Pastel pencils are a lovely medium for this subject, as the pigments can be blended both optically and physically. Look carefully at the scene and you will be amazed at how many different greens and yellows you can discern. Here, the artist has created an impression of the stems blowing in the breeze. Note how the warm, orangey yellows in the foreground make this area seem closer to the viewer.

Mediterranean seascape

This tranquil scene of waves lapping a Mediterranean shore is full of sunshine and light. Although the composition is simple there is plenty to hold the viewer's attention, from the partially submerged rocks in the foreground through to the town in the distance.

The main interest, of course, is the rippling sea itself, with its myriad tones of blue, green and even violet – and soft pastels are a wonderful medium in which to portray this. It's surprising how many colours you can see in the water. Water takes its colour from objects in and around it – the sky, rocks, seaweed and algae, and so on – so look at the surroundings, as well as at the water, as this will help you assess which colours are required. Half-close your eyes when you look at the scene, as this makes it easier to assess the different colours and tones. It's hard to be precise about which colours to use in this project, as soft pastels are available in such a huge range of colours, but put together a selection of blues, greens, violets and browns, from very pale to very dark.

Remember that the rules of both linear and aerial perspective apply to sea and sky just as much as they do to objects on land. Distant waves, for example, appear smaller than those close at hand. Colours also appear lighter with distance and texture is less pronounced – so smooth out your pastel marks on the sky and the most distant part of the sea by blending them lightly with your fingers or a clean rag.

Observe your seascape very carefully before you draw. Look at any sea scene for a while and you will see that the waves follow a regular pattern, with incoming waves building to a peak and then falling back. Note how high they go and how far back they fall when they break around a rock or crash on to the shoreline.

Materials
- *Cream pastel paper*
- *Neutral brown or grey pastel pencil*
- *Soft pastels: a selection of blues, greens, blue-greens, turquoises, violets, browns, oranges, ochres and white*
- *Soft rag*

The scene
The dark wall on the left forms a diagonal line at its base which directs the viewer's attention towards the town in the distance. The town itself is positioned roughly 'on the third' – a strong position in any composition.

1 Using a neutral-coloured pastel pencil, put in the lines of the headland and horizon and the dark, submerged rocks in the water. Note that the artist decided to make the headland and rocks more prominent in the scene and omitted the light-coloured concrete walkway in the bottom left of the reference photo.

2 Roughly block in the sky with a mid-blue pastel and blend with a clean rag to smooth out the marks.

Tip: Keep the coverage slightly uneven, to give some texture to the sky. If the colour is completely flat and uniform, it will look rather boring.

3 Block in the wall on the left with a mid-brown pastel and smooth out the marks with a rag or your fingers. Scribble in the partially submerged rocks using the same colour.

4 Block in the sea using a turquoise pastel, leaving some spaces for the breaking wavelets. Note that the sea has some areas that are lighter than others, so apply less pressure here.

5 Apply a few light touches of a darker turquoise to the darkest parts of the sea in the background. Loosely scribble jade green over the foreground water to pick up the green tones, varying the amount of pressure you apply to get some variety of tone.

6 Looking carefully at their rough, uneven shapes, apply burnt orange over the tops of the exposed rocks in the sea near the base of the wall, switching to a reddish brown for their bases. Blend the marks gently with clean fingertips.

▶

7 Look at the colours in the water. The underside of breaking wavelets contains some surprisingly dark greens and blues. Stroke these in lightly, making sure your strokes follow the direction in which the waves are moving. Gently smooth the marks a little with your fingertips – but don't overdo the blending, as allowing some of the underlying paper colour to show through helps to create a sense of movement in the water.

8 Continue building up different colours in the water, using dark greens and blues and dots of light spring green.

Tip: Remember to keep referring to your reference photo. It's easy to get carried away with building up the colours and forget to look at the shades that are actually there.

Assessment time

There is a lovely sense of movement in the sea and a good range of different tones and colours. However, the rocks themselves are nothing more than flat blocks of colour and need to be made to look three-dimensional.

The wall is a flat expanse of brown – it needs to look rough in texture and three-dimensional.

The rocks are little more than patches of colour and lack form.

9 Start to build up some tone and texture on the wall by scribbling on dark greens and browns, making horizontal strokes that suggest the blocks that it is built from. Smudge the colours with your fingers, allowing some of the underlying mid-brown that you put down in Step 3 to remain visible.

10 Repeat the process on the rocks surrounding the partially enclosed still pool, scribbling a reddish brown over the orange to build up the form. On the distant headland, put in the darkest colours of the buildings – the browns and terracottas of the roofs. Apply pale yellow ochre to the white of the headland so the paper doesn't look so stark.

11 Dot some light and mid-toned olive greens into the headland for the distant trees. Apply pale blue and mid-tone turquoise over the sky to darken it towards the top (skies generally look paler close to the horizon).

12 Although little detail is visible in the distant town, you need to give some indication of the buildings. Look for the dark tones under the eaves of the roofs. Making small horizontal strokes, apply pale blues and greens over the most distant part of the sea and smooth them out with your fingers. Apply thin lines of dark brown around the bases of the partially exposed rocks.

13 Having now given the rocks some solidity, return to working on the foreground seascape again, and put in the white of the wavelets as they break around the partially exposed rocks. Use the tip of the pastel and dot in white here and there around this area. The softly lapping sea has only a gentle swell, so take care that you don't make the wavelets too big.

14 Continue adding texture to the foreground sea, making sure that the dark greens, blues and purples in this area are dark enough. Don't smooth out your marks too much: it is important to have more texture in the foreground of a scene than in the background, as this is one way of creating a sense of recession.

15 Continue building up form on the exposed rocks, using a range of dark oranges and browns as before. It is now time to put in the final touches – more tiny strokes of white for the breaking wavelets and horizontal strokes of dark greens and blues in the foreground sea, wherever you judge it to be necessary.

The finished drawing

There is a lively sense of movement in the sea: one can almost feel the ebb and flow of the waves and hear them lapping around the rocks. Note how allowing some of the paper to show through the pastel marks creates the effect of sunlight sparkling on the water. There is just enough detail in the distant headland for us to know that there is a town there; more detail, however, would draw the viewer's attention away from the sea in the foreground and destroy the illusion that we are looking almost directly into the sun, our eyes dazzled by its brilliance.

The wall provides solidity at the edge of the picture area and helps to direct the viewer's eye through the scene.

Small horizontal strokes of blues, greens and purples are used to convey the many different shades in the water.

Detail diminishes with distance, and so the pastel marks in this area of the sea are smoothed out to give less texture.

Snow scene

Here's an interesting challenge: how do you draw a bright, white subject such as snow using charcoal, which is one of the densest and darkest drawing mediums available? The answer is not to attempt to draw the snow at all: allow the white of the paper to stand for the brightest parts of the snow and use the charcoal for the mid- and dark tones. Focus your attention on the clumps of earth that poke up above it and the thicket of trees on the right of the image, rather than on the powdery, white covering on the ground.

Also, note that the snow is not a uniformly pure, unsullied white. The ground undulates, forming little peaks and shaded troughs. Tones of grey are required to make this distinction – smooth, pale tones without any sharp edges. To give the drawing impact, you also need to contrast the heavy, solid forms of the trees and background ridge with the much softer and less substantial shapes of the clouds and shadows. Use all the blending techniques at your disposal: smudge lines with your fingertips or (for larger areas) the side of your hand, or blend marks with a torchon, a sponge or a piece of tissue paper, as this allows you to build up areas of tone without creating a hard line.

If you get accidental charcoal smudges, don't worry. This is an unavoidable part of charcoal drawing and you can always wipe off powder with an eraser. A kneaded eraser gives a soft, smooth finish; for sharp edges, cut a plastic eraser or pull a kneaded eraser to a fine point. For an cheaper alternative, try small pieces of soft white bread.

The scene

Here is a typical winter scene across a ploughed field. The thicket of trees on the right provides a focal point while the clumps of earth poking up through the snow form diagonal lines across the field that lead the viewer's eye through the composition.

Materials
- *Smooth drawing paper*
- *Willow charcoal sticks – thin and medium*
- *Kneaded eraser*
- *Compressed charcoal stick*
- *Large torchon*
- *Plastic eraser, cut to give a sharp edge*
- *Small sponge*

1 Using a thin charcoal stick, map out the proportions of the scene. Look for specific points from which you can measure other elements. Here, the artist used the clump of trees as a starting point. When he measured it, he discovered that the distance from the base of the clump to the base of the ridge in the distance is roughly the same as the distance from the base of the trees to the base of the image.

2 Using the side of the charcoal, roughly block in the wedge-shaped area of land in the middle distance and the thicket of trees on the right. Make jagged, spiky marks for the top of the thicket to convey the texture of the trees. Note also that some areas are darker in tone than others; although you will elaborate this later, it's a good idea to get some tonal variation into the drawing even at this early stage.

3 Using the tip of a medium charcoal stick, draw the darkest areas within the thicket of trees. Look for the negative shapes – the spaces between the branches rather than the branches themselves. Switch to a thin charcoal stick for the branches that stick out at the sides and top of the main mass. Using a kneaded eraser, lightly stroke off charcoal for the lighter-toned branches within the clump.

4 Start to introduce some form into the wedge-shaped area of land in the middle distance. The trees at the front of this area are very dark in tone, so build up the tone with heavy, vertical strokes. Use a thin charcoal stick to start dotting in the exposed clumps of earth peeping up above the snow in the field and make thin vertical strokes for the grasses on the right-hand side of the image.

5 Using a stick of compressed charcoal, put in some very dark blacks in the trees in the middle distance so that you gradually begin to build up texture and tone. Also use the compressed charcoal to draw more of the exposed clumps of earth that run across the field, making small, dotted marks of varying sizes and making the marks darker as you come towards the foreground.

6 Rub some charcoal on to a scrap piece of paper and press the end of a large torchon into the resulting powder. Gently stroke the torchon over the snow that leads down to the clump of trees to create soft shadows.

7 Using a plastic eraser, wipe off some of the charcoal to create the snow on the edges of the fields in the middle distance. By cutting the eraser you can get a crisp, sharp-edged line.

Assessment time

The main elements of the composition are in place, but the contrast between the sky (to which no charcoal has been applied so far) and the dark, dense tones of the trees is too extreme. Even so, the thicket of trees on the right still needs to be darkened in places. Your task now is to develop texture and tone across the whole image. In order to do this, you will need to continually assess the tonal balance of the drawing as a whole, to ensure that no one part becomes too dominant.

As yet there is no detail in the sky, which forms roughly half the image.

With the exception of a few foreground shadows, there is no texture or detail in the snow areas.

▶

8 Wipe the side of a medium stick of charcoal over the sky area. Note how the coverage is uneven, creating lovely dappled marks.

9 Using a circular motion, vigorously rub a small sponge over the sky to smooth out the charcoal marks.

10 There is a band of blue in the sky above the land and below the mass of clouds. Block this in using the side of a medium charcoal stick and blend it to a mid-grey with a torchon, making it darker in tone than the rest of the sky. Using a kneaded eraser and a vigorous circular motion, lift off shapes for the looming storm clouds. Don't worry about the tones within the clouds at this stage; just try to get the approximate shapes. Note how putting some detail in the sky has changed the mood of the drawing from a tranquil winter scene to something much more dramatic, in which the threat of a storm is imminent.

11 Put in some very dark storm clouds and blend the charcoal with your fingertips or a sponge. Immediately, the scene looks much more dramatic; note how the dark areas of sky balance the thicket of trees on the right of the image. Scribble some charcoal on a piece of scrap paper to get some loose powder, as in Step 6. Dip a torchon in the powder and gently stroke it over the sky to create softly blended areas of mid-tone between the clouds. This allows the white areas of the clouds to stand out more clearly.

12 The sky is now quite dark, so you may need to darken the land mass to make it more dominant. Compressed charcoal gives a very rich, intense black. Note how the snow also seems to sparkle and stand out more once the land mass has been darkened.

13 Using a thin charcoal stick, put in any remaining exposed clumps of earth on the field. Re-assess the whites in relation to the rest of the image. You may need to use a kneaded eraser to lift off some charcoal in the grasses on the right.

The finished drawing

This drawing demonstrates the versatility of charcoal. It can be blended to give a smooth, even coverage, as in the mid-toned areas of the sky, or used to create bold, highly textured marks, as in the clump of trees. The success of the image is due largely to the contrast between the very light and the very dark areas. In scenes like this, the key is often to darken the dark areas rather than to lighten the lights.

Charcoal is softly blended with a sponge to create the clouds.

The exposed clumps of earth are paler in the distance, creating a sense of recession.

'Drawing' some of the branches with an eraser creates fine, crisp-edged lines.

Reflections in rippling water

Shimmering reflections are great fun to draw. Perfect reflections, however, do not necessarily make the most interesting subjects, as part of the fascination lies in seeing how familiar shapes and objects are distorted when reflected. In this project, your challenge is not only to draw the reflections convincingly but also to capture a sense of movement in the gently rippling water.

Before you start drawing, spend time looking at both the shapes and the sizes of the ripples. There are two distinct types of ripple in the scene – horizontal ripples, which are caused by a very slight breeze, and circular ripples in front of the ducks as they move through the water. Look out for these shapes and alter your pencil strokes accordingly, using a curving or swirling motion for the circular ripples. And remember the rules of perspective: in order to create a sense of distance, foreground ripples need to be larger and further apart than those in the background.

Coloured pencils are used for this project – the perfect opportunity for you to practise optical colour blending. The water, of course, takes its colour mainly from the trees and foliage on the bankside – and even though the trees are not actually included in this scene, you need to provide enough information

for the viewer to be able to infer something of the country park setting.

The first stage is to colour in the background. This makes it easier to gauge how to treat the birds. If you were to colour the birds first, you could easily find that you'd made them too dark – an irreversible mistake. When you're drawing white objects, remember that they are never pure white, even though our eyes perceive them as such. Some shading, however slight, is essential for them to look three-dimensional.

Materials
- *Smooth drawing paper*
- *Coloured pencils: turquoise-green, range of greens, yellow, dark blue, pale blue, violet, light orange, dark red*

The scene
Placing the birds almost in the centre of the image helps to create a calm, peaceful mood that is appropriate to the subject. The rippling water adds interest to what might otherwise be a fairly bland scene.

1 Using a turquoise-green pencil, outline the ducks and their reflections and indicate the main ripples. If you're worried about colouring in the birds when you start to work on the water in Step 2, use masking fluid for the outlines.

2 With green and yellow pencils (yellow for the right-hand side, which receives a little more light than the rest of the scene), lightly colour in the water around the birds, using a zig-zag motion to echo the shape of the ripples.

3 Apply more yellow over the lower half of the water, below the birds, and dark green behind them, again using a zig-zag motion of the pencil and leaving some gaps so that the underlying colours remain visible. Note that the water that lies between the birds is very dark indeed, so you can afford to apply a little more pressure with the pencil here.

4 Apply dark green in front of the birds. Now that you've established much of the base colour of the water, you can begin to create more of a sense of movement – so switch from a zig-zag motion to curved marks and swirls to capture the ripples. Remember the rules of perspective: make the foreground ripples larger and further apart than those in the background.

5 In areas where the foliage is reflected in the water, apply more yellow over the green, still using curved marks and swirls to maintain the movement of the ripples in the water. Apply dark blue in the very darkest areas – particularly under the birds. Remember to maintain an even but light pressure so as not to give too much emphasis to one particular area.

Assessment time
The water takes its colour from the things that are reflected in it – the trees on the bankside. Already we can see a range of colours, but the water is still too light overall. We are also beginning to get a feeling of movement, as the ripples flow outwards from the birds, and this needs to be enhanced. Finally, of course, the birds themselves need to be drawn in detail – something that is much easier to do now that we have a clearer idea of how dark the darkest areas need to be.

6 Using a pale blue pencil and horizontal strokes, lightly put some shading on the birds' white feathers.

Curved pencil marks create the ripples in the water.

The water needs to be darker overall, but the base colours have been established.

7 Using a violet pencil, lightly hatch over the blue to darken it slightly. Lightly indicate the position and angle of the birds' eyes.

▶

8 Continue working on the foreground water, putting in dots and dashes of violet, bright green and yellow. Keep referring to your reference photo to see where the yellow highlights, which are formed where the lightest bits of foliage are refected in the water, occur and what shape and size the ripples need to be.

9 Darken the water with a dark blue pencil, still using zig-zag and swirling motions so that you don't lose the ripples and the sense of motion in the water. By bringing the blue right up to the birds, you can sharpen their outlines. Colour in the beaks and reflections with a light orange and overlay with dark red on the lower beaks.

10 The divide between the birds and their reflections is not clear. Gently stroke dark green over the reflections to subdue them and push them back into the water. Using a dark blue pencil, draw around the backs and necks of the birds so that they stand out from the water.

11 Adjust the colours in the water until you feel you've got the balance right; it helps to take a short break from the drawing at this point, as it will enable you to look at your work more objectively. Make sure the darkest parts are dark enough (add more blue if necessary), and that the yellows are not too bright (yellow ochre is a less harsh alternative). Note that the reflections are broken by the ripples in the water – but the overall shapes are still very clear.

The finished drawing

By using curved and zig-zagging pencil strokes for the ripples, the artist has created a lovely sense of movement in the water. Note that the ripples are larger in the foreground than in the background, which helps to create a sense of distance. The reflections are slightly broken by the ripples and more subdued in colour than the birds themselves.

The artist has also made the scene slightly sunnier than it was in reality, by using brighter colours and including more yellow. Although the birds are centrally placed in the picture area, the two birds on the left have their heads turned towards one another, which helps to draw our attention in to the centre of the scene.

The reflections are broken by the ripples and more subdued in colour than the birds.

The angle of the birds' heads directs our attention to the centre of the scene.

The foreground ripples are larger than those in the background.

Landscape on a large scale

Drawing on a large scale is very liberating, both physically and mentally. Physically, it allows you to use the full stretch of your arm and hand to make bold, sweeping marks that are full of energy. Mentally, you have to simplify things and stop yourself getting bogged down in unnecessary detail. Try to get back to the essence of the scene – the aspects that made you want to draw it in the first place.

Charcoal is the perfect medium for a project such as this, as it is so versatile and easy to apply. You can drag the side of the charcoal across the support to cover large areas quickly, blend it using a variety of techniques, or use the tip to make expressive, linear marks.

If you can't find sheets of purpose-made drawing paper large enough, a roll of lining (liner) paper from a DIY store makes an inexpensive alternative. Pin it to a drawing board (or attach it with masking tape), and then place the drawing board on a studio easel or hang it on a wall.

The composition of large-scale drawings needs careful thought and planning. Before you embark on the actual drawing, it's a good idea to make a schematic sketch of the composition, working out where the centre of interest falls and making sure that the viewer's eye is led to that point.

Materials
- *Drawing paper 1 x 1.25m (3 x 4ft)*
- *Charcoal: thick and thin sticks*
- *Kneaded eraser*

The scene
The rocky escarpment is surmounted on the left by a wooded area that echoes the bands of trees at the base of the escarpment and in the fields below. A narrow track leads the eye into the scene along the line of trees and up to the rocks.

1 First, decide how much of the scene you want to include in your drawing and map out the positions of the main elements. To make this process easier, divide the scene into quarters (either mentally or by making light marks at the edges of the paper) and mark out where things fall in each square. Use light marks at this stage, just to establish where everything goes. Lightly block in the slope of the cliff to give yourself a visual guide to where to position the trees that stand at its base.

2 Work out where the darkest areas of tone are going to be and roughly block them in with a thick charcoal stick. The wooded mass on the top of the cliff is very dark, so you can apply a lot of pressure to the charcoal for this area. However, it's not a solid, straight-edged wedge shape: look closely and you will see that the tops of the trees are gently rounded. Outline the trees at the back of the fields with light dots and dashes, then block them in with the side of the charcoal stick.

3 Turn your attention back to the cliffs and look for differences in tone: the contrasts between dark, shaded gullies and crevices and the more brightly lit areas that are in full sunshine give the cliffs some sense of form. Block in the larger areas of tone using the side of the charcoal stick and moving your whole arm, not just your hand, keeping the coverage fairly uneven so that some of the paper texture shows through. Note that the brightest areas are barely touched by the charcoal. Continue blocking in the band of trees at the back of the fields, putting in nothing more than generalized shapes at this stage.

4 Outline the trees at the base of the cliff, then sketchily develop some tone within them. Note the number of different shapes – the tall, elongated cypress trees and the more rounded shapes elsewhere. Start to put in some jagged, linear marks on the cliff to create some texture.

Tip: Continually check the size of the trees and the distances between them and other elements of the scene. It's very easy to make the trees too big and destroy the scale of the drawing.

5 Finish outlining the shapes of the band of trees that runs across the middle of the drawing. Now you can begin to develop the foreground a little. Put in the foreground grasses, using both the tip of the charcoal and the side.

Tip: Work across the drawing as a whole, rather than concentrating on one area. This makes it easier to get the tonal balance of the drawing right.

6 Continue working on the trees in the middle of the drawing, concentrating on the overall shapes. Add more tone to the trees at the base of the cliff so that they begin to stand out more. Using the tip of the charcoal, put in more jagged, linear marks on the side of the cliff. These dark fissures help to create a sense of form and texture.

▶

Assessment time

Details in the image are taking shape, but it requires much more tonal contrast and texture. The trees are little more than generalized shapes at this stage and do not look truly three-dimensional; you need to develop more tone within them and also to put in the shadows that they cast. We are beginning to see the different facets of the cliff, but the darkest marks are not yet dark enough to give us any real sense of form.

Very little work has been done on the foreground. It is too bright in relation to the rest of the image.

The linear marks on the cliff need to be developed further to create a sense of form.

The foreground grasses are too indistinct. More texture is needed here.

7 Very gently stroke the side of a thin charcoal stick over the foreground to create some tone and texture. Note how using the charcoal in this way gives a slightly uneven coverage. Press slightly harder on the charcoal to put in the sides of the track that zig-zags its way through the scene. Also indicate the shadows cast by the trees.

Tip: Smooth out the long cast shadows with your fingertips, in order to make them less textured than the trees themselves.

8 Very gently make a series of horizontal marks over the fields immediately below the cliff, pulling the full length of the charcoal stick over the paper to create the effect of ploughed furrows. Using the tip of the charcoal and pressing down firmly, put in the dark trunks of the trees in the centre of the image.

9 The trees are now taking real shape. Look at how the light catches them. Darken the shaded sides, using the side of the charcoal to create broad areas of tone. Immediately the trees begin to look more three-dimensional as you add the shadows they cast. Developing this tone takes them away from generalized shapes.

10 Using a kneaded eraser, gently lift off some of the charcoal from the side of the trees that catches the light. If you lift off too much, simply go over the area in charcoal again. Using the tip of a thin charcoal stick, introduce more texture into the foreground grasses by making crisp, dark, vertical marks.

The finished drawing

Working on a large scale has allowed the artist to use the full stretch of his arm to make bold, sweeping marks that give the drawing a very energetic, lively feel. He has concentrated on the essentials of the scene, rather than trying to put in every single detail, but his clever use of tonal contrasts gives the image a convincing sense of form. The foreground track leads our eye through the scene to the trees and cliff beyond – a classic compositional device.

Note how the contrasts between light and dark areas reveal the different facets of the cliff face.

Detail diminishes with distance; the amount of detail that we can discern in the grasses tells us that they are in the foreground.

Lifting off charcoal from the most brightly lit sides of the trees shows us which direction the light is coming from.

Rocky canyon

This is one of the best-known and most distinctive of all landscapes in the USA – Bryce Canyon in south-western Utah. The colourful rock formations, a series of eroded spires, are best viewed in early morning and late afternoon, when they glow in the sunlight.

When you're drawing formations such as these, look for tonal contrast within the rocks as this is what shows the different planes and makes it look three-dimensional. If a rock juts out at a sharp angle, there is a clear transition from one plane to another and the difference in tone between one side and another is very obvious. If the rock is smooth and rounded, the transition in tone is more gradual.

Drawing the many fissures and crevices also shows the form of the subject. If the shadows in these crevices are very deep, you might be tempted to draw them in black – but black can look very stark and unnatural. Instead, use a dark complementary colour for the shadows – so if the rocks are a reddish-brown, as here, try opting for a purple-based shadow colour.

Materials
- *Pastel paper*
- *Thin charcoal stick*
- *Soft pastels: pale and dark blue, grey, violet, browns, cadmium orange, pale pink, greens, yellow ochre*
- *Clean rag or kitchen paper*
- *Kneaded eraser*
- *Conté stick: brown*
- *Blending brush*

The scene
Trees in the foreground provide a sense of scale: without them, it would be hard to estimate how tall the rocks are.

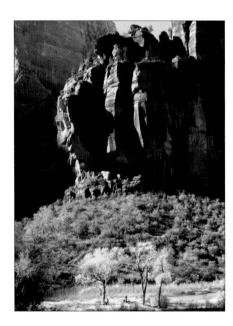

> **Tip**: If you're working from a photograph, you may find that it helps to grid up both the photograph and your drawing paper and then work systematically one square at a time until all the elements are in place.

1 Using a thin charcoal stick, draw the rock formations and lightly indicate the main areas of shade. Using the side of a pale blue pastel, block in the small patch of sky that is visible above the rocks.

2 Using a cool grey pastel on its side, block in the darker, shaded areas of the rock formations. This gives the rocks some form and establishes the direction from which the light is coming.

3 Using a violet pastel on its side, put in the strata of the background rock-face. Note how the diagonal lines within this rock-face reveal the structure and add drama to the composition.

4 Again using the side of the pastel, strengthen the horizontal strata on the background rock, applying light blue at the top of the rock and a darker blue at the base.

5 Begin applying colour to the rock formations, using brown and dark violet in the shadow areas, using the edge of the pastel to define the divisions between the sections. The crevices between the rocks are dark and deep: a deep violet provides the necessary dark tone and is a warmer and more lively colour than black.

6 Apply cadmium orange to the rock formations. On the shaded facets, where the orange is overlaid on the violet, a rich optical colour mix ensues. On the more brightly lit parts of the landscape, the orange represents the naturally warm, sun-kissed colour of the rock. The colour combination is sympathetic but striking.

▶

Assessment time
The structure of the rock formations is beginning to emerge, but the contrast between the shaded and the more brightly lit facets is not yet strong enough. The rock formations also need to be brought forwards in the scene, so that they stand out from the background cliff.

The main rock formations look rather flat.

It is hard to tell that this cliff is some distance behind the main rock formations.

7 Lightly apply pale grey and pink over the foreground scrubland. Use grey for the shaded areas and pink for those illuminated by the late-afternoon sunlight.

8 Apply touches of pale green to the scrubland, then soften the whole area by blending the colours with a clean rag or piece of kitchen paper, using a gentle circular motion.

9 Using a kneaded eraser, wipe off the shapes of the trees in the foreground. If you accidentally wipe off too much, simply repeat Steps 7 and 8 for the right background colour.

10 Draw the trees, using a brown Conté stick for the trunks and their shadows, and bright green to roughly block in the masses of foliage.

11 Wipe a clean rag or a piece of kitchen paper over the top of the background rock-face and the sky to lift off excess pastel dust and soften the colour.

 Tip: Turn the rag round in your hand so that you don't smudge violet over the sky.

12 Soften the violet on the lower part of the background rock-face by using a blending brush, brushing it both horizontally and vertically. If you haven't got a blending brush, you could use your fingers or a torchon, but the bristles of the brush create very fine lines in the pastel dust, which are perfect for the striations in the rock. Although this rock-face is in the distance, it is important to create some subtle texture here.

13 Add more detail to the main rock-face, using the side of the deep violet pastel to overlay colour and the tip to draw on short horizontal and vertical lines to emphasize the different facets within the rock.

14 Now start working on the foreground scrubland. Using a pale green pastel on its side, roughly scribble in the base colour of the scrubby bushes that cover the ground immediately below the rock-face.

15 Build up the foreground foliage, using a range of pale and mid-toned greens and grey-greens. A general impression of the shapes is all that is required. Put in the roadway with a warm ochre pastel.

16 Define the edges of the roadway in brown. Also add a range of browns to the scrubland, using jagged, vertical strokes of dark brown for the thickest stems and branches. Make sure your pastel strokes follow the direction of growth.

The finished drawing

This colourful drawing captures the heat and the mood of the scene very well. Warm oranges and purples predominate and are perfectly suited to the arid, semi-desert landscape. The artist used bold linear strokes to capture the striations and jagged texture of the rocks and the drawing is full of energy. Although some texture is evident on the background cliff, blending out the pastel marks in this area has helped to create a sense of recession. For the foreground scrubland, the artist opted for an impressionistic approach, describing the overall shapes and textures with dots and dashes of greens and grey-greens. This contributes to the liveliness of the scene and concentrates attention on the rocks, which are the main point of interest.

As the background cliff is less textured, it appears to be further away.

The trees are dwarfed by the rocks that tower above, and give a sense of scale.

Tonal contrasts reveal the different facets of the rocks.

Quick sketches of still lifes: Potted plant

Although we normally think of a still life as being an item, or a group of items, that the artist has deliberately arranged, there are also what are known as 'found' still lifes, which are things that the artist has come across by chance.

As with any subject, you need to think about your viewpoint and position carefully. If the object is heavy, it may not be possible to move it – but you can easily adjust your own position to give a more pleasing composition. Your eye level is important, too: in the examples shown on these two pages, the artist's eye level was above the plant, enabling her to look inside the pot and see how the leaves grow out of the main stem. If the pot had been at eye level, so that she was looking at it horizontally, this kind of information would have been hidden from view.

The background is also an important element of a still life and you need to decide how to treat it. One of the delights of drawing and painting is that you have the freedom to interpret things as you wish, and to omit or alter things that you do not like. If you find that the background detracts from the subject, or prevents the subject standing out clearly, simplify it to a tonal wash.

The scene
Here, the artist discovered a potted plant in a corner of a friend's garden and was intrigued by the sculptural shapes of the leaves and the arching shadows that they cast on the gravel beneath the pot.

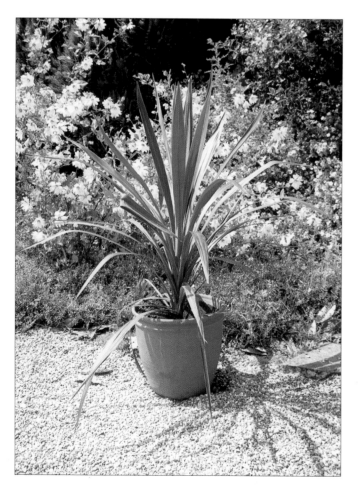

5-minute sketch: graphite pencil
In a five-minute sketch, you can only explore the basic shapes of the subject. Looking at the negative shapes can be a great help when you are drawing objects that are irregularly shaped. Here, the artist blocked in the negative shapes on the left with loose scribbles, as this made it easier to see the shapes of the leaves themselves. A context and three-dimensional feel were also suggested by sketching in the cast shadow.

10-minute sketch: graphite pencil and water-soluble sepia ink
In this sketch, the artist explored ways of treating the background, using both washes of water-soluble ink between the leaves to provide a dark background and loose pen-and-ink shapes to imply the presence of other plants.

15-minute sketch: graphite pencil, water-soluble sepia ink and water-soluble pencils

The plant itself was treated in the same way as in the 10-minute sketch, opposite. While the ink was still damp, water-soluble pencils were used to add detail on the pot and shadows. As the paper was damp, the colours spread.

25-minute sketch: graphite pencil, masking fluid, water-soluble sepia ink and water-soluble pencils

Here, masking fluid protected some of the daisy-like flowers in the background from the washes of ink. When the other details were complete, the masking fluid was removed and the centres of the flowers drawn in with an orange water-soluble pencil.

Quick sketches of still lifes: Patio table

Still lifes can sometimes benefit from a helping hand. If you find a potentially interesting subject, take time to think about ways you might improve on it. You could perhaps rearrange the different elements so that they make a more balanced, or a more dynamic, composition. Look at the spaces between the objects, as well as at the objects themselves, and experiment with different combinations, adding or removing items until you are happy with the way things look. Also think about the relative scale of the objects: although you can create some dramatic images by extreme contrasts, it is usually better if the items in a still life are on a similar scale.

When sketching glassware, remember that it takes on the colour or tone of objects around it. Look at the background and at nearby objects before you sketch the glass itself. Against a pale background, the edge may not be entirely visible. For example, look at the glass on the left in the sketch below.

The scene

The artist was attracted by the lovely dappled light on the table and the colourful gourds and grapes, but felt that something was missing. She decided to add the two glasses of wine to provide some extra colour and to introduce a vertical element into the composition. They also give the still life more of a story, implying that the cut grapes will be made into wine later.

5-minute sketch: water-soluble sketching pencil

Once she was sure she had drawn the ellipses of the glasses correctly, the artist blocked in tone for the red wine, paying careful attention to the highlights reflecting off the glasses in order to convey their smooth shininess. The shadows on the metal table were created by brushing clean water over the water-soluble pencil marks, providing an effective contrast with the linear marks used for the hard glass.

15-minute sketch: chalk and charcoal pencil

In a scene full of contrasts such as this, where there are very bright highlights and dense shadows, it often helps to use a toned ground so that you can start from a mid-tone. Here, the artist worked on dark-blue pastel paper to create a simple but effective tonal study. White chalk was used for the wrought-iron chair and table, with the side of the chalk being used for the tabletop and the highlights scribbled in with the tip of the chalk. The darkest elements of the still life – the bottle, glasses and fruit – were sketched in charcoal pencil.

15-minute sketch: ballpoint pen

For this sketch, the artist removed some of the grapes to give a less cluttered arrangement and positioned the glasses on opposite sides of the table to create a more balanced composition. Although you cannot vary the width of the lines you make with a ballpoint pen, you can create a surprisingly wide range of marks and tones by hatching and cross-hatching. Note how the tones range from the very dark fig on the right to the very bright tone of the table in areas where no shadows are cast. Note, too, how shading the background allows the lines of the white wrought-iron chair on the left to stand out.

30-minute sketch: oil pastel

To create the reflective surface of the wrought-iron table, the artist applied colour with oil pastels and softened the marks with a rag dipped in turpentine.

Quick sketches of still lifes: Old tools

Still lifes don't have to be 'pretty'. Functional items, such as old tools, kitchen utensils or garden implements, can make a graphic composition. The more time you spend working out the arrangement, the better. Think about the relative scale of the objects: something like a tiny nut or bolt will simply have no impact if it's placed next to a large object such as a mechanical vice or other large industrial tool. Think about the background, too: it's generally best to go for something fairly neutral, which doesn't detract from the subject. A plain, painted wall or a scratched wooden workbench, grimed through years of use, will both make good backgrounds for this kind of still life.

The set-up
Here, the artist selected a few battered items from his workshop and set them up against a plain white background to allow the shapes to stand out clearly. He chose three items of similar size, as odd numbers of items tend to work compositionally. The composition is well balanced, with both the scraper and funnel placed 'on the third'.

5-minute sketch: charcoal
Here, the artist began by outlining the shapes of the objects before blocking in the darkest areas, such as the reflection of the old bottle in the metal scraper, with the side of the charcoal stick. He then smudged the marks on the scraper and funnel with his finger to soften them and create the effect of a smooth, metallic surface. Note how the charcoal is applied roughly and unevenly, helping to convey the texture of the rather battered funnel and bottle.

15-minute sketch: ballpoint pen

You can't cover large areas quickly with a ballpoint pen, so any subject that requires a lot of shading, as here, is likely to take longer. Here, the shaded areas were hatched, with the lines being drawn closer together or even cross-hatched for the darkest sections. As always with a subject such as this, it is essential that you observe the highlights accurately in order to convey the form; it's easy to get so engrossed in the rather mechanical and repetitive business of shading that you lose sight of the drawing as a whole.

30-minute sketch: pencil

As in the ballpoint pen sketch, above, the artist made use of hatching to shade the darkest areas – but the beauty of using a soft pencil is that you can combine linear work (to outline the shapes and get crisp edges) with softly blended areas that convey the smooth metallic surfaces. The result is a less mechanical-looking sketch than the ballpoint pen version shown above. And, with more time at your disposal, you can concentrate on subtle changes in tone that convey the somewhat pitted surface of the funnel and bottle.

Exotic flowers

Many exotic flowers are readily available from good florist's shops. They are wonderful things to draw and make a simple still life to set up at home. The bright yellow or orange flowers of *Strelitzia* burst out of a boat-shaped bract like head feathers on an exotic bird, giving rise to one of the flower's common names – the bird of paradise flower.

This project gives you the opportunity to exploit the potential of soft pastels. The colours are vibrant and perfectly suited to this subject, and soft pastels have a smooth texture which is ideal for the flowers and leaves. The bold, graphic shapes of the flowers and leaves require strong, flowing marks, which can be easily blended.

Materials
- *Paper or board*
- *Soft pastels: pale green, yellow ochre, bright yellow, greyish green, reddish brown, dark green, grey, pale pink, ultramarine blue, cadmium yellow, cadmium orange, bright green, vermilion, deep red, Naples yellow*
- *Hard pastel: cadmium red*
- *Pastel pencil: Hooker's green*
- *Rag or kitchen paper*

The set-up
The flowers were placed in a tall glass vase, with the leaves acting as a dark background. The vase does not form part of the final drawing, but it keeps the flowers upright.

1 Using a pale green soft pastel, map out the main lines of your subject, including the main veins of the two large leaves.

2 Put in the main veins of the leaves with a yellow ochre pastel. Use a bright yellow and a greyish green pastel for the *Strelitzia* bract, smoothing out the join between the colours with your fingers. Outline the leaves in reddish brown (the colour will barely be visible in the finished drawing, but the edge of the leaves needs to be clearly defined).

3 Draw the veins on the background leaf in the same reddish brown. Fill in the spaces between them with a dark green, using the side of the pastel. Repeat the process on the foreground leaf, using yellow ochre for the veins and filling in the spaces in grey.

Tip: Don't press too hard: you want some of the texture of the support to show through.

4 Outline the individual *Strelitzia* flowers in pale pink and the tongues in ultramarine blue.

5 Fill in the flowers in cadmium yellow and cadmium orange soft pastel, and define the line between the petals with a cadmium red hard pastel.

6 Blend the flower colours with your fingertips to give a smooth, waxy texture, making sure you don't pull any colour on to the background.

7 Use a Hooker's green pastel pencil to define the tiny triangular areas of leaf that lie between the bases of the flowers.

8 Block in the stem of the *Strelitzia* flower with a light, bright green, overlaid with a little cadmium yellow in places for the highlights. Block in the rest of the background leaf in dark green, using the side of the pastel.

9 Leaving the brightest highlights in the drawing untouched for the moment, block in the red flowers with vermilion and ultramarine blue. Use ultramarine blue for the dark, shaded parts of the flowers.

10 Still working around the highlights, overlay deep red on the ultramarine blue to create a rich, almost black, red. Carefully blend the colours on the leaves with the side of your hand or a clean rag, smoothing out the pastel marks to give a waxy finish to the leaves. Work on one section at a time, making sure you retain something of the linear marks of the veins.

Tip: The highlights are an important part of the picture, so observe their shape carefully. They show us how glossy the surface is and tell us which direction the light is coming from.

11 Using the side of the pastel, apply dark green to the foreground leaf between the veins to begin to add texture to the plant.

12 The leaves are firm and waxy in texture, so blend the dark green with your fingertips to get a smooth, even finish.

13 Using the side of the pastel, apply pale Naples yellow over the white background so that it does not look so bright and stark.

The finished drawing

This is a vibrant and colourful drawing that exploits the characteristics of soft pastels to the full. They are the perfect choice for this subject: the colours are very vibrant and the thick sticks ideal for covering large areas, while blending the marks creates the smooth, almost waxy texture of the flowers and leaves. Note how the foreground leaf is lighter and more textured than the background one, which helps to bring it forwards in the image.

Soft blending of the marks makes the veins an integral part of the leaf.

The warm yellow background complements the orange flowers, which look striking against the dark green of the leaves.

The untouched white highlights reveal the direction of the light.

The sharp tip of a pastel pencil is used for small areas where precision is required.

Metal detail

In this project, coloured pencils are used to draw the distinctive Rolls-Royce 'Spirit of Ecstasy' motif, creating a smooth, metallic-looking sheen. As always with this kind of detailed coloured-pencil work, you need to put down a number of very light layers of pigment. If you apply too heavy a layer, the wax in the pigment clogs up the tooth of the paper so subsequent layers of colour will not go on as smoothly or as evenly.

Try to maintain an even pressure, using the side of the pencil so that the coverage is perfectly smooth and there are no obvious pencil marks. You can get away with a few imperfections when you are drawing a more uneven surface, but not when you are trying to convey perfectly smooth metal.

It is also very important to assess the tones carefully. The figurine is smooth and rounded, and it's sometimes hard to work out exactly where changes in tone occur – but these changes in tone are the only real clue you have to the form of the object. Look for a darkening of tone as the figure curves away from the light. It happens so gradually that it may seem barely perceptible when you first look at a subject like this, but at some point a darkening does occur and you need to render it in your pencil work.

The surface is also highly reflective. There are many different facets in the figurine, so you don't see complete reflections in the same way that you would in a flat plate-glass window, for example. Nonetheless, the green of the foliage and the red of the car can be seen in the silver of the figurine. Details like this, tiny though they may be, add verisimilitude to your work.

Materials
- Smooth, heavy drawing paper
- HB pencil
- Craft (utility) knife and cutting mat
- Masking film (frisket paper)
- Kitchen paper or clean rag
- Coloured pencils: bottle green, olive green, mineral green, scarlet lake, gunmetal grey, blue-grey, burnt umber, indigo, geranium lake, deep vermilion

The subject
The viewpoint has been chosen so that the head and wings of the 'Spirit of Ecstasy' figure stand out against the dark background foliage and the distinctive Rolls-Royce logo is clearly evident.

2 Using a craft knife, shave tiny slivers of pigment off a bottle-green pencil over the foliage background. Repeat with olive and mineral greens so that you get a number of shades of green in the foliage. Finally, add a few flecks of scarlet lake; a complementary colour to the green, this gives more variety to the foliage and provides a subtle visual link with the colour of the car bonnet.

1 Using an HB pencil, lightly sketch the car indicating the main area of mid-tone within it. Using a craft knife on a cutting mat, cut a mask out of masking film to place over the metal figurine and the car bonnet (hood). Peel off the backing paper and stick it in place, smoothing out any wrinkles by rubbing over it with a piece of kitchen paper or a clean rag.

3 Take a piece of kitchen paper, scrunch it up, and gently wipe it over the pencil shavings to blend them on the paper. This is an effective way of covering a large area quickly.

Tip: Make horizontal strokes. This creates a streaked effect, which gives the impression of movement.

4 Remove the mask. (You may need to use the tip of a craft knife to lift up the edge.) Alternating between a gunmetal grey and a blue-grey pencil and using very light strokes, put in the darkest parts of the metal figure. You may find it easier to assess the tones if you half-close your eyes.

5 Continue the process on the base of the figurine and the top of the radiator grille, still using very light strokes. Note that some of the foliage is reflected in the metal towards the back of the base; put this in using whichever greens you feel are appropriate.

6 Go over the lettering in gunmetal grey. Block in the most deeply shaded parts of the radiator grille in burnt umber, then overlay indigo in the same area. The optical mix creates a richer, more varied colour than you could achieve using only black.

7 Using a scarlet lake pencil and horizontal strokes, apply the first thin layer of colour to the car bonnet, leaving the very brightest highlights untouched. Where there is a change of plane, define it with a slightly heavier pencil line.

8 Go over the scarlet with geranium lake. With the application of this second layer, the colour is beginning to look closer to the way it should look, as the two reds mix optically on the paper. The coverage is also more dense and is beginning to take on a metallic sheen.

▶

Assessment time

The red section of the car needs to be more intensely coloured. Go over it again with a deep vermilion pencil. We can see how smooth the metallic front and top of the car is, but it does not yet look shiny enough. We are beginning to see the different planes of the image, but more differentiation is needed between them. Building up the layers of a coloured-pencil drawing is a slow, meticulous process that needs to be done.

The figure needs to be darkened very slightly.

The front of the bonnet needs to be darkened, so that it is obvious that it lies on a different plane to the top of the bonnet.

More layers of red are needed to achieve a really smooth, deep sheen on the bonnet (hood) of the car.

The radiator grille is too pale; more tone is needed here.

9 Apply a light layer of gunmetal grey to the thin metal strip that runs along the length of the bonnet, behind the figurine. This strip catches the light, so only a little colour is needed. Overlay very pale olive green on the rounded end, which is slightly in shadow. Darken the tone on the front of the radiator panel with a blue-grey pencil, using the side of the pencil rather than the tip.

10 Re-assess the tonal values of the picture as a whole, reinforcing the darks wherever necessary. Also continue building up the red of the bonnet, alternating layers of scarlet lake and geranium lake, until you reach the right density of colour.

The finished drawing

In this drawing the metalwork looks so smooth that you almost feel you could reach out and touch it! The artist has paid very careful attention to the highlights and shadows, as these are what convey the form of the object and make it look three-dimensional. She has built up the colour by applying several thin layers, allowing them to mix optically on the support to create a rich finish. You could put more detail into the background if you wish, but this simple approach allows the subject to stand out.

The plain background allows the subject to stand out.

Bright highlights on the figure tell us which direction the light is coming from.

Variations in the density of the red convey the curve of the bonnet (hood).

Still life with garlic and shallots

Try to get into the habit of drawing every day – even if it's only for ten minutes during your lunch break. One of the most wonderful things about drawing is that you can create images anywhere, from anything that you have to hand. Paper clips and a pencil sharpener from your desk at work, a piece of fruit that you're going to eat for your lunch, a coffee cup or a few children's toys – anything will do, so long as you spend time observing and drawing.

The project shown here is a good example of this approach. The artist constructed a simple still life using nothing more than a wooden chopping board, a bulb of garlic and a couple of shallots from the kitchen. For drawing equipment, he deliberately restricted himself to just two graphite pencils and a torchon. It's well worth setting yourself an exercise like this one, as limiting the number of drawing tools that you use allows you to experiment and become familiar with the range of marks that each one can create. Here, for example, the torchon is used not only to blend graphite marks but also to 'draw' soft marks that add an interesting texture to the image.

No doubt you've heard it before, but we make no excuse for repeating it here: odd numbers of objects (three, five, seven) invariably make more satisfying still-life compositions than even numbers. When you're setting up a still life, look at how the objects relate to one another. Look at the overall shape that the assembled objects make, as well as at the shape of each item within the group. Remember that the spaces between them are, compositionally, as important as the objects themselves, as are any shadows. Try different viewpoints: the spatial relationships will change if you look down on (or up at) your subject. Above all, try out different arrangements until you find one that seems to work.

Materials
- *Smooth drawing paper*
- *Graphite pencils: HB and H*
- *Torchon*
- *Kneaded eraser*

The set-up
Shadows almost always make a scene more interesting, as they allow you to exploit the differences between the light and the shaded areas of your subject. Here, the artist set up a table lamp to one side of his still life, so that the objects cast strong shadows to the left of the image.

1 Lightly sketch your subject. Start from the base of the garlic stalk and work outwards: this will enable you to establish the relative positions and sizes much more easily than an outline drawing would. Lightly shade the darkest areas of the garlic bulb and indicate the cast shadow to the left. Use a torchon to blend the graphite and create smooth areas of tone. Also use the torchon to 'draw' the individual cloves of garlic.

2 Using an H pencil, outline the shallot on the right and its papery stem. Start to shade underneath the garlic bulb and put in the deep area of shadow that lies between the garlic and the shallot. Using the side of the pencil, begin shading the darkest side of the shallot. Try to make sure your pencil strokes run in the same direction as the striations in the skin of the shallot.

3 Working downwards (and making sure you keep within the outline), smooth out the graphite on the shaded area of the shallot with a torchon.

4 Using an H pencil, draw the veining on the papery outer covering of the garlic. Put more shading on the dark areas of the garlic and smooth out the marks with a torchon.

6 Reinforce the twisting line of the garlic stalk, using an irregular, slightly broken line which helps to convey the texture.

5 Outline the stalk and the lower part of the shallot on the left, where it cuts across behind the garlic, and shade in the underside of the shallot. Lightly hatch in more of the shadow cast by the garlic and blend with the torchon. (Shadows need to look considerably less substantial and solid than the objects that cast them.) Make sure, however, that you retain the crisp line around the edge of the garlic so that there is a clear distinction between it and the shadow; if necessary, reinforce the outline.

7 Using an HB pencil, put in the linear detailing around the top of the stalk of the shallot on the left. It almost looks like a small claw reaching forwards.

▶

8 Shade the stalk of the shallot on the left and darken the shadow underneath. Use the torchon to 'draw' soft horizontal lines across the shallot, and then the H pencil to put in sharper, linear marks on the shallot's papery covering.

9 Shade the left-hand side of the garlic stalk, which is furthest away from the light. Note how the stalk twists and turns, and is irregular in width; convey this in the way that you shade it.

Assessment time

The drawing is progressing well, but the objects do not stand out clearly enough in relation to each other or to the shadows. More tonal contrast is needed, as is more contrast of texture.

The shadow is almost as strong in tone as the object that casts it.

The stalks of both the shallot and the garlic are not strong enough.

10 Extend and darken the shadows cast by both the garlic and the shallot on the left. Blend the marks to a soft shadow using a torchon.

11 Darken the shaded areas of the shallot on the right and complete the linear detailing on the garlic. Clean off any smudges with a kneaded eraser.

The finished drawing

Objects in this still life are not particularly interesting in themselves, but they have been carefully arranged so that the stalks lead our eye around the picture in a circle. The soft shadows anchor the subjects on the surface. The artist used a range of pencil techniques, from crisp linear detailing on the stalks to soft shading using the side of the pencil, and smooth blending of the graphite using a torchon. He also used the torchon as a drawing tool in its own right, to put in the segments of the garlic that can be seen under the papery outer covering. The result is a simple but effective still life.

The shadow has been blended and softened so that it appears less substantial than the object that casts it.

Linear details, such as this split in the covering of the shallot, add a contrast in texture.

These subtle striations in the papery outer covering of the garlic are made by 'drawing' lines with the torchon.

Still life with pears

Fruit is ideal for still-life drawings, with simple shapes and subtle textures and colours that are perfect for rendering in coloured pencil. Select fruit that is not over-ripe, as any blemishes will soon start to deteriorate and you will be in a race against time to complete the drawing before the fruit starts to shrivel. This particular project uses slightly under-ripe pears with smooth surfaces that have a few marks and blemishes to add texture, and a soft blush of warmth on the skin. To keep the arrangement simple, the artist placed the pears on a plain, dark-blue background which contrasts effectively with the pale-green fruit and adds depth to the shadows.

The key to the success of this drawing is to work slowly, carefully building up the tones and textures of the fruit with gentle pencil marks. The depth and range of colours found on the pear skins are achieved through several layers, starting with the lightest tone and adding light pencil strokes on top, with any spots or blemishes added at a later stage to enhance texture and emphasize the rounded shapes. When working with a group of objects, keep checking their relationships and use their cast shadows to create a convincing visual link.

Materials
- *Smooth drawing paper*
- *HB pencil*
- *Coloured pencils: pale yellow, bright green, warm yellow, olive green, dark brown, raw umber, burnt umber, pale brown, bronze, mid-brown, mid-blue, dark blue, rich dark blue, ultramarine blue*
- *Eraser*

The set-up
A rich blue fabric background complements the yellow-green of the pears. Try out different arrangements to find what works best. Here, the shadows cast by the foremost pear add interest to the composition. The foremost pear is also laid on its side so that we can see the dimpled base, adding variety to the composition.

1 Using an HB pencil, lightly sketch the outlines of the pears, making sure you allow enough space on either side for the folds in the background fabric. Map out the positions of the stalks and the corresponding base on the pear at the bottom right of the composition. To make it easier, look at the angle of the stalk. This helps you to establish the central axis that runs all the way through the fruit.

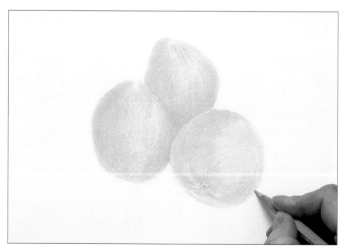

2 Very lightly apply a layer of pale yellow over all the pears, including the highlight areas. Apply a bright green over the green areas of the pears, using gentle pressure and loose strokes. Reapply the pale yellow and then add a warmer yellow, such as Naples yellow, around the edges of the back pear where it is tinged with pink. Use the same colour where the cast shadow falls on the middle pear.

3 Start to build up tones to develop the form of the pears. Use a combination of pale yellow and bright green on the foreground pear to add the darker tones. Use loose strokes when applying the bright green so that the underlying yellow shows through. Combine pale yellow and an olive green to fill in the colour of the stalks, using darker browns, such as raw umber and Vandyke brown, on the shadow side. Use the same browns to sketch in the details of the dimple at the base of the foreground pear, using olive green for the darker areas of skin surrounding it, and a dark brown such as burnt umber for the darkest areas.

4 Continue gradually building up the colours and tones on the foreground pear. Use loose, light scribbles of olive green to develop a sense of texture as well as colour. To give an impression of the rounded form of the fruit, apply the strokes in the same direction as the curves.

Tip: Don't make the stalks too dark at this stage, as they will need to stand out against the background.

5 Next, build up the colours and texture on the background pear. Use pale brown to define the edge where the foreground pear overlaps it, then apply loose, even strokes of the same colour, following the form of the pear. Work around the highlights and add a light layer of bright green with a slightly darker brown on top. Define the outer edge in olive green to ensure that it will stand out against the background. Add a hint of a warm pink glow by combining bronze and mid-brown on the lower half of the pear, fading out to a soft edge on the shadow area. To bring all the colours together, apply a layer of pale yellow.

6 Finish the back pear by adding green along the edges where the shape curves. Use short marks to add texture, avoiding the highlight areas. Emphasize the shadow with light touches of dark brown. Start to build up the colour on the middle pear, with an olive green for the area of shadow cast by the foreground pear, following the form of the pear with more upright, vertical strokes. Add brown along the edges with yellow over the top to knock it back. With a dark brown, such as Vandyke brown, add the details at the base of the stalk, using tiny strokes to follow the contours of the recess to give the impression of a dip. Add any tiny blemishes or rough patches of skin using the same dark brown.

Tip: Use a sheet of tracing paper beneath your hand to protect the lower half of the drawing.

▶

Assessment time

At this stage the pears appear to have form and texture, defined by the light highlights and the darker shadows. To complete the subtleties of the pears' skin colours, you need to build up more layers of pale yellow and green.

Fill in around the highlights to finalize their shape with a light yellow. Use mid- to dark browns to add any blemishes or areas of rough skin, keeping the pencil marks light.

Work over all the pears with a final layer of yellow and a little olive green on the darker tones. You can then start to add in the blue background; this will be a long, slow process, as you need to apply several layers, but it's worth taking your time over it in order to achieve the right density of colour.

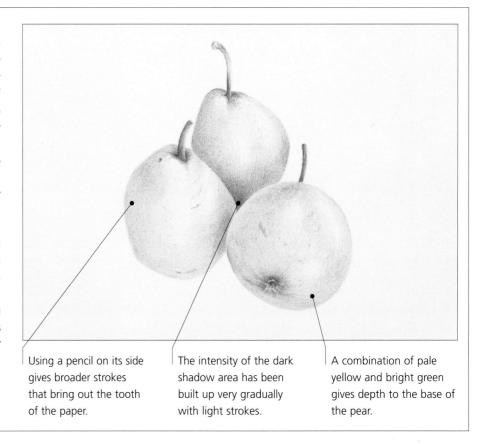

Using a pencil on its side gives broader strokes that bring out the tooth of the paper.

The intensity of the dark shadow area has been built up very gradually with light strokes.

A combination of pale yellow and bright green gives depth to the base of the pear.

7 Start to add the blue background using a mid-blue, such as Prussian blue, applied with very light strokes using the tip of the pencil. Try to achieve an even layer of colour with no variations, working from the outside in to the edge of the pears for better control. Turn the drawing as you work, but keep the pencil strokes running in the same direction.

Tip: Use a soft eraser, or a piece of reusable putty adhesive, to soften or remove any hard edges along the folds.

8 Using a slightly darker blue, continue to build up the colour, mapping out the folds of the material. Roughly sketch in the edge of the long vertical fold on the left, a soft diagonal fold in the lower right-hand corner, and swathes of fabric in the top right-hand corner. To emphasize the way the fabric is draped, build up the colour on the shadow side of the folds using strokes that follow the drape. Build up the shadows at the base of the pears with the same colour, to establish a visual link between the pears and the background fabric, and apply a crisp line around each pear with a very sharp pencil point.

9 With a dark, rich blue, such as indigo, start to intensify the colour of the background, applying more pressure in the deepest shadows. To accentuate the folds, build up colour on the edge of the fold, turning the paper if necessary to follow the direction of the curve. Where the light hits the top of the fold leave a lighter edge, using a rich blue such as ultramarine with a mid-blue underneath. The lines of the folds should give a sense of the weight of the fabric and the effect of gravity. Use a very dark blue in the darkest shadow areas between the two foreground pears and the recessed fold on the left.

The finished drawing

With the background completed, an intensity is added to this subject which brings the pears to life. The pleasing composition is enhanced by the subtle effect of the contrasting colours of blue and green. To ensure that the pears aren't overshadowed by the rich blue of the fabric, the artist reassessed the whole drawing, adding more strength to the fruit to reinforce any light areas. The stalks and blemishes or shadows on the top of the pears were also redefined with a dark brown to give them a crisper edge, and the texture of the skin was further highlighted with some additional speckles.

The folds of fabric are created by leaving a bright highlight with soft edges that blend to a deep blue in the recess of the fold.

A dark brown has been used to define the stalks so that they stand out against the blue background.

The brown speckles on the fruit are closer together on the edges to give the impression of rounded form.

Small objects drawn large

This project, which uses everyday household objects such as keys, nuts, bolts and screws, is easy to replicate at home and produces a graphic, contemporary-looking image that would look wonderful hung on a plain white wall.

The point of the exercise is two-fold. First, although the arrangement appears random, when you set it up you really have to think about the negative shapes in the composition – that is, the spaces between the objects. Compositionally, the spaces help the viewer's eye to move through the composition to alight on the positive shapes – that is, the metal objects themselves.

Second, this is an exercise in loosening up and freeing both your eye and your hand. When you are drawing small objects, there is sometimes a tendency for your hand to tighten up as you try to put in every tiny detail, and this can make a drawing look very dull and lifeless. Drawing things larger than life size, as here, forces you to move your hand and your wrist as you work, producing a looser, freer image. It also makes you look at your subject in a different way: you're more likely to view the composition as a whole, instead of getting bogged down in individual items, and to concentrate on the overall shapes and how they relate to one another.

To give you some idea of the scale involved, the large key towards the bottom of the image was about 7cm (just under 3in) long in reality, whereas in the finished drawing, it is about 15cm (6in) long – so the objects were drawn at roughly twice life size.

Materials
- *Smooth drawing paper*
- *Thin charcoal stick*
- *Charcoal pencil*
- *Kneaded eraser*

> **Tip**: To make the measuring easier, imagine lines running horizontally and vertically through the composition and work out where the small household objects intersect them.

The set-up
Scatter your chosen objects loosely on a white background, such as a large piece of paper or a white tablecloth. You'll find you get a better result if you just throw the objects down and see what shape they make rather than attempting to place each one precisely – although you'll almost certainly need to spend time creating the right balance and adjusting the positions before you start drawing. To create some modelling on the objects, place a table lamp to one side.

1 Using a thin charcoal stick, map out the shapes, carefully measuring both the objects and the spaces between them. Here, the artist decided to allow some of the objects to disappear off the edge of the paper, as she felt this created a more dynamic image than keeping everything within the rectangle of the paper.

2 Using the side of the charcoal stick, block in the shapes of the shadows cast by the objects and smooth out the charcoal with your fingers. Putting in the shadows helps to give the objects solidity.

3 Gradually begin to refine the shapes of the objects, sharpening the edges with darker, linear marks. Blend the marks with your fingers, as before, to create the smooth, metallic finish.

4 Continue refining the shapes. This is a gradual process, but the objects soon begin to 'emerge' from the paper as three-dimensional forms.

5 Using the tip of the charcoal, introduce some detailing, such as the threads of the screws and the notches on the keys. Work across the drawing as a whole, so that you can continually assess each object in relation to its neighbours.

6 Continue the process of refinement and detailing. The process is akin to a photographer zooming in on his or her subject: initially you're looking at just the overall shapes, but as you add detailing the subject pops into sharper focus.

▶

Assessment time

The shapes of the objects and their shadows are in place, but they still look rather indistinct. The edges, in particular, need to be more clearly defined. Overall, the tone is too uniform. Increasing the contrast between the dark and the light areas will make the objects look more three-dimensional.

Much crisper detailing is required on some objects.

Although the basic shape is there, some objects are too pale and lack the contrast that is needed to make them look realistic and three-dimensional.

7 Working over the drawing as a whole, continue defining the edges of the objects and blending to create smooth, metallic surfaces.

8 Use the tip of a charcoal pencil to sharpen up the edges of the objects and put in very fine details such as the screw threads.

9 The chain is one of the few objects that look rather indistinct. Define the edges with the charcoal pencil, observing carefully how the links are connected. Remember to note where the highlights fall on the chain and allow the white of the paper to show through here. Clean up any smudges with a kneaded eraser.

The finished drawing

This is a graphic and realistic drawing that shows how even the most humble of objects has potential as an artistic subject. The composition has been carefully planned: note how all the objects are placed diagonally on the paper so that they lead the viewer's eye into the picture. Although all the objects are small, some, such as the bolt and pencil sharpener, are deeper than others and cast shadows that add interest and another texture to the image. Crisp, linear marks and soft blending of the charcoal combine to depict the hard-edged metal objects and the smooth surfaces.

The cast shadows reveal that some objects are deeper than others.

The highlights on the twisted metal chain reveal the direction of the light.

Blending charcoal with the fingers creates a smooth texture.

Quick sketches of buildings: Church façade

Drawing a façade is a good way to start sketching buildings as, since you're only dealing with one side, there is no need to get involved in the complications of two-point perspective. Here, the light and shade on the building and the lovely rough texture of the stonework provide plenty of interest. Beware of putting in too much textural detail, though, as it can make a drawing look dead and lifeless; a suggestion of the texture in a few key parts of the image is normally sufficient.

These sketches were made in pen and ink, or pen and ink plus water-soluble pencils. Pen and ink is a popular choice for architectural studies, as fine lines are often required. Ink is difficult to erase if you make a mistake – so it's a good idea to start in pencil and then reinforce the lines in pen once you're sure the measurements and proportions are correct. Though the water-soluble pencils were used dry on this occasion, blending the colours of the stonework with water would be very effective without destroying the textural pen-and-ink work.

The scene
This viewpoint offers several possible compositions: the façade of the church, the details of the arches on the left, and even textural studies of the stonework.

5-minute sketch: pen and ink
With a relatively simple shape like this church, you should be able to map out the basic structure of the building in a matter of minutes. The key, of course, is to measure all the elements and their relative positions very carefully. A thumbnail sketch like this is a good warm-up exercise when you're drawing on location. It also gives you the chance to work out the composition of a larger drawing.

10-minute sketch: pen and ink
In ten minutes, you have time to indicate the texture of the stonework and the heavy wooden door. A few simple pen lines are enough to show the shape of the stones set into the walls; don't overdo it or you'll deaden the overall effect. A sketch made *in situ* like this provides very useful reference material for a larger drawing that you can work up in more detail at a later date.

15-minute sketch: pen and ink, plus water-soluble pencils

Here, the artist decided to concentrate on the arches to the left of the church. With a little more time at your disposal, you can explore the effects of light and shade and try to capture more of the texture and character of the stonework. As in the other sketches on these two pages, the basic composition was mapped out in pencil before any pen-and-ink work was done, with hatched pen lines indicating the most deeply shaded parts of the scene. Finally, water-soluble pencils were used to block in the colour of the stonework. Sketches such as this are a very good way to explore the tonal relationships in a scene.

25-minute sketch: pen and ink, plus water-soluble pencils

This is a more elaborate version of the sketch above, and shows the relationship between the church and the ruined building next to it. The artist was able to get closer to the true colours of the scene, using warm, purplish blues for the shadow areas. There was also time to place the building in a setting by including trees and foreground grass.

Quick sketches of buildings: Doorway

Old, dilapidated buildings provide a great opportunity to practise sketching different textures. Crumbling stonework and tiles, sun-bleached wood with the grain exposed, worn carvings: all are full of texture for the artist. And if the building happens to be in an exotic location, so much the better. When it comes to capturing the essence of a foreign country, architectural styles are as evocative as costumes or landscapes. Look for interesting details when you're on your travels. You'll be amazed at how effectively a few quick sketches made *in situ* can bring back memories.

When you are sketching textures, do not put in too many details or they will dominate the image. Imply the textures rather than putting in every single brick and crack. Allow the shapes and textural contrasts to speak for themselves.

The scene
Coming across this doorway into a courtyard in Beijing, China, the artist was attracted by the contrast between the rather grandiose entrance and the much more humble-looking abode within. Although the subject is almost monochromatic, it provided enough visual interest to prompt her to make a few quick sketches.

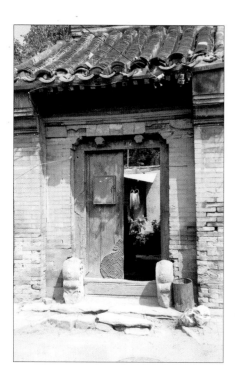

5-minute sketch: charcoal
In this sketch, the artist has managed to create a convincing impression of depth through her use of tone. Strong linear marks for the shaded undersides of the arch and doorway combine with smudged charcoal for the shadow areas. The artist has put in just enough linear detail to hint at the shapes of the bricks and roof tiles, without detracting from the tonal study.

Tip: If you don't measure up carefully, the proportions will look wrong – particularly if you can see two sides of the building and want to use two-point perspective. Imagine lines running horizontally and vertically through the image and work out where the different elements, such as a window, or a decorative detail such as a door knocker, intersect them.

15-minute sketch: pen and ink, plus brush

Overlapping roof tiles make an attractive graphic study. Here, the scratchy, irregular lines produced by using a dip pen seem appropriate for the rather rough-textured, hand-made tiles. The artist wanted to retain the lines of the tiles, so she drew them in waterproof ink before applying a dilute wash of ink over the top for the shadow areas.

25-minute sketch: pastel

This sketch is built up of blocks of colour and tone which get progressively lighter the nearer they are to the foreground of the scene. The tooth of the paper helps to convey the texture of the stonework.

30–40 minute sketch: pencil and graphite

Having explored the composition of the scene and some of the textures in the previous two sketches, the artist then settled down to making a more detailed sketch. She used a 6B pencil for the darkest parts, including the deep cracks in the bricks on the right, and a graphite stick (blended with a torchon) for the areas in shadow. Note how much of the brickwork is left untouched: nonetheless, the texture is conveyed very effectively.

Quick sketches of buildings: Farmhouse

A viewpoint that shows two sides of a building almost inevitably creates a more interesting drawing than one that shows only the front façade. It also allows you to exploit contrasts of light and shade, as one side will be more brightly lit than its neighbour. Bear in mind the rules of two-point perspective. You can plot the perspective lines to their vanishing points if you wish, but careful observation and measuring are generally sufficient.

5-minute sketch: 2B pencil

Here, the artist drew the farmhouse from a slightly higher eye level than that from which the photo on the right was taken. As a result, the front façade of the house is virtually square on and the line of the roof does not slope downward. When you're drawing a building, it's well worth making a quick sketch such as this simply to measure and check the placement of the different elements.

The scene

In this winter scene, the dark hedge in front of the building and the skeletal trees by the side stand out well against the snowy ground and provide a contrast of texture with the flat stonework. The hedge also echoes the shape of the building, as the lines of the hedge run more or less parallel to the building's sides. In this instance, the artist chose to make a series of monochrome sketches – but the bright red door and little outbuilding or porch would provide an uplifting splash of colour in a study made in coloured pencil or chalk.

15-minute sketch: burnt umber coloured pencil

When you've established the basic lines of the composition, you can begin to explore the tonal relationships in more detail. Here, we've shown the tonal study as a separate sketch; in reality, you might choose to make this the second stage of the sketch shown on the opposite page. The artist has also begun to put some detail into the stonework, being careful not to overdo things and deaden the overall effect.

30-minute sketch: ballpoint pen

Although only the cornerstones are drawn in any detail, the artist has nonetheless created the texture of the building very well by means of simple shading. One of the most common mistakes that beginners make is to underestimate the tonal range in a scene; make sure that the darkest areas, such as the window recesses, are really dark, as this will make the snow-covered areas really sparkle. The brightest parts, such as the roof, can be left virtually untouched.

Old wooden gateway

There is something very appealing about drawing distressed wood and peeling paint. Rusting nails and bolts, differences in tone where the sun has bleached and faded the paintwork, the grain and texture of the wood underneath – all these things are far more interesting to look at than a pristine, gloss-painted surface. Perhaps part of the fascination is that, as the paint begins to peel away, we catch glimpses into the past and a hint of how the subject once looked.

Soft pastel is a lovely medium to use for a project such as this. By using the pastel on its side and lightly applying a thin layer of colour that does not completely cover the paper or a previous layer of pastel (a technique known as scumbling), you can create wonderful textures and optical colour mixes. By blending the pastel with your fingertips, you can produce smooth textures and even tones.

This particular scene is also a study in light and shade. The bright patch of sunlight that can be seen through the gateway is balanced by the area of shade to its left, with the wedge-shaped shadow helping to lead the viewer's eye through the scene to the buildings at the back of the courtyard.

A drawing of the gateway alone might result in a soulless study of an architectural detail: by including the yard, we can speculate about the daily routine and living conditions of the inhabitants and bring the scene to life. However, too much emphasis on it would detract from the gateway, so subdue the detail and draw the buildings as blocks of colour.

Materials
- *Terracotta-coloured pastel paper*
- *Soft pastels: reddish brown, black, white, pale mint green, dark mint green, greys, browns, yellow*

The scene
This old wooden gateway, covered in peeling paint and bleached by the sun, offers both interesting textures and colours and an intriguing glimpse into the courtyard beyond.

1 Using a reddish brown pastel on terracotta-coloured pastel paper, lightly sketch the main lines of the scene – the arch of the gate, the wooden panels, the roofline and the division between the shaded and sunlit parts of the ground that can be seen through the gate. The terracotta paper enhances the feeling of warmth and sunlight in the scene; it also provides the base colour both for the buildings in the courtyard and for the wooden gateway, which means that the paper does part of the work for you, without you having to apply the base colour separately.

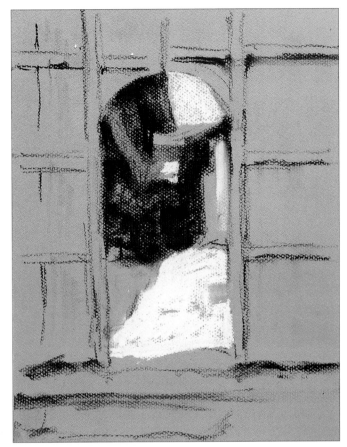

2 Using the side of a black pastel, block in the buildings. Note the differences in tone: some areas, such as the underside of the overhanging roof, are darker than others. Add the thin shadows cast by the wooden panels on the gate.

3 Using the side of a white pastel, block in the very bright highlight areas of the sunlit foreground and the sky above the building, as well as those parts of the building that receive the most light.

4 Using a pale mint green pastel (again using the side rather than the tip), block in the painted gateway. Allow some of the paper to show through so that it looks as if an earlier colour is showing through the peeling paint: with this kind of subject, it's important to keep the coverage loose and uneven so that you create the right kind of texture.

5 Use a reddish brown pastel to put in some of the exposed wood on the gateway, rubbing with your fingers to smooth out the colour. Roughly scumble a darker mint green over the paler green in places, allowing some of the lighter colour to show through. The successive layers of pastel help to develop more depth and texture on the gate.

▶

6 Stroke pale mint green followed by reddish brown over the foreground and blend the colours with your fingertips. Allow some of the mint green to remain visible: some parts of the foreground are cooler in tone than others.

Assessment time

Although the buildings in the courtyard are little more than blocks of colour, we can see the different facets: paying careful attention to the light and dark tones makes them look like three-dimensional forms. A little more depth of colour is needed on the gateway, as too much of the paper texture is visible.

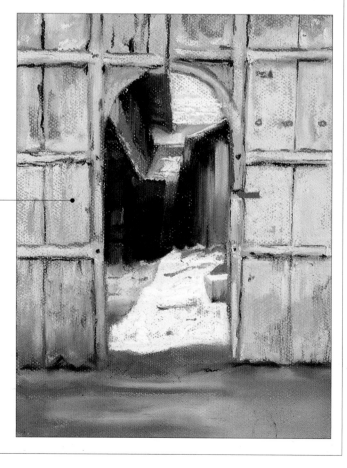

The paper texture is too prominent; this area does not look like painted wood.

7 Block in the shaded part of the ground in the yard with pale grey and white, blending the colours a little with your fingers but taking care that they retain their individuality. Reinforce the different facets of the courtyard buildings using mid-browns and greys for the shaded sides and applying light touches of white, smoothed out with your fingers, for the more brightly lit parts and the shafts of light.

8 Apply light vertical strokes of mint green, with tiny touches of yellow, over the individual panels of the gate and blend with your fingers. Remember to allow a little of the paper colour to show through, to give the impression of underlying layers of paint.

The finished drawing

This drawing exploits two important soft pastel techniques – scumbling and finger blending. The main focus of interest is the sun-bleached, painted gateway, which forms a natural frame for the scene of the courtyard beyond. Although detail is subdued and the buildings are little more than blocks of colour, there is a delightful sense of light and shade in the scene. The shafts of sunlight, which are created by stroking a thin line of white pastel across the paper, are balanced by blocks of shadow, so neither one dominates.

The arch of the gate is positioned almost centrally in the picture space, which creates a calm mood. However, this is balanced by the lines of the buildings and the wedge-shaped patches of sunlight and shadow, which help to break the symmetry and make the composition more dynamic.

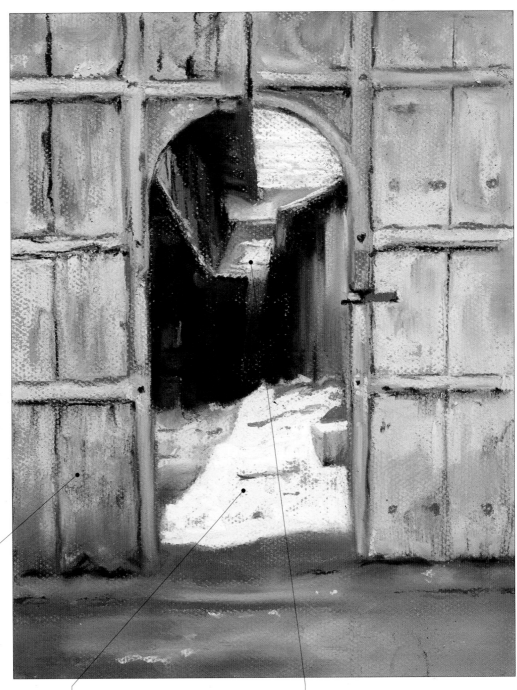

Scumbling allows the paper colour to show through and, at the same time, suggests the texture of the wood.

The bright, wedge-shaped patch of sunlight leads our eye through the picture to the buildings at the back of the courtyard.

Blocks of tone – light versus dark – reveal the form of the buildings and the direction from which the light comes.

Venetian building

This project is an exercise in perspective. The bottom of the balcony is more or less at the artist's eye level – so this is the horizon line. If you look at the initial pencil sketch in Step 1, you will see that the artist has drawn the bottom of the balcony to form a straight, horizontal line across the centre of the image. Any parallel line above this point (such as the line of the roof) will appear to slope down towards the vanishing point, while anything below it (such as the base of the building) appears to slope upwards. Take time over your initial pencil sketch to make sure you get the angles and proportions right. Texture is important, too, and the rough texture of the ancient brickwork is very pleasing to the eye. Don't try to draw every single brick, as this would make the image too 'busy' and detract from the overall effect. Leaving some areas empty gives much-needed contrast of texture and implies the smooth render that would once have covered the whole façade of the building.

Pen and ink is an ideal medium for architectural drawings, as it allows you to make very precise marks. Here, both permanent and water-soluble inks are used, creating a combination of crisp, linear details and ink washes, which soften the overall effect. For this project, the artist chose to use sepia ink, rather than black, as it is a much softer colour and helps to give the drawing a rather nostalgic, old-fashioned feel.

Materials
- *Heavy drawing paper*
- *HB pencil*
- *Permanent and water-soluble sepia inks*
- *Steel-nibbed pens*
- *Fine paintbrush*
- *Gouache paint: white*

The scene
Old buildings such as this one, with the canal lapping at its foundations, are common in Venice, and can evoke a strong sense of the past. The decorative lines of the balconies are not overly ornate, but they hold our interest, and the beautiful arched doors and windows form a repeating pattern that runs through the whole image.

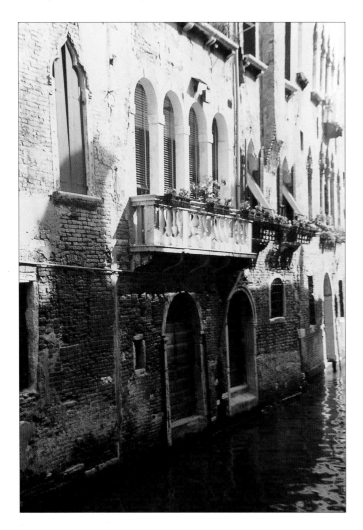

1 Using an HB pencil, make a light, detailed sketch of the scene, making sure you measure all the different elements.

 Tip: The buildings are receding. Put in the perspective sight-lines as a guide; you can erase them later.

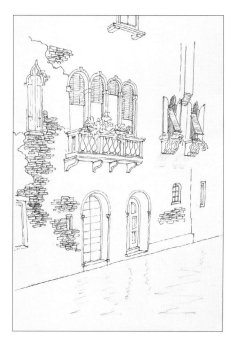

2 Following your pencil lines and using permanent sepia ink, carefully ink in the windows and balconies. It is very important not to use water-soluble ink here, as you want to retain all the crisp detail of these lines in the finished drawing.

3 Continue with the ink work, using water-soluble sepia ink for the foliage and brickwork. Also hatch the windows behind the open shutters on the top right of the drawing in water-soluble ink, drawing the lines close together as this area is very dark.

4 Continue working on the brickwork, alternating between permanent and water-soluble sepia inks. Put in the lines of the Venetian blinds in permanent ink. Here the artist has put the blinds in at different heights to add interest.

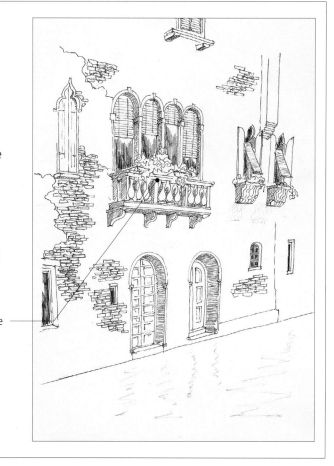

5 Using water-soluble ink, put in some light hatching around the window recesses, in the windows below the blinds, and under the balconies to introduce some shading. (The ink will be washed over at a later stage, so that the hatching marks blend together to create an area of solid tone.)

Assessment time
The main lines are now in place. However, although there is some indication of the shading around the windows and balconies, the image overall looks rather flat and two-dimensional. From this point onwards, concentrate on creating more depth and texture.

Although there is some texture and detail, the image as a whole is rather lifeless. Washes of colour will help to counteract this.

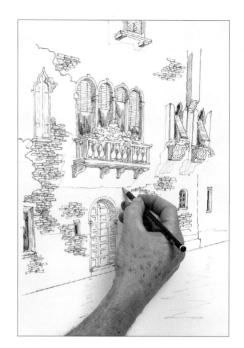

6 As the light is coming from the right of the scene, the balconies cast oblique shadows on the façade of the building. Put them in lightly, using an HB pencil. (The pencil lines act as a positional guide – they should be covered up by washes of ink later.)

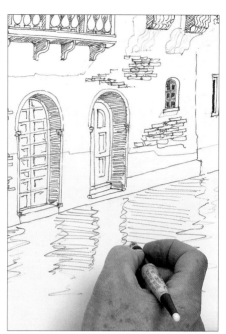

7 Using permanent ink and zig-zagging vertical lines, draw the ripples in the water. Hatch the darkest areas of the water, using water-soluble ink. The ripples will remain visible when a wash is applied, while the hatching will blend to an area of solid tone.

8 Erase all the remaining pencil lines, apart from the cast shadows that you put in in Step 6. Load a paintbrush with water and brush over the shaded parts of the building. The lines drawn in water-soluble ink will dissolve, allowing you to create areas of solid tone.

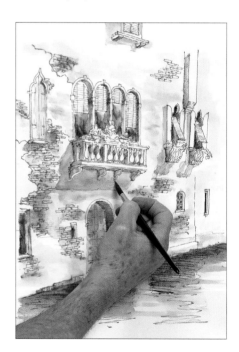

9 Continue brushing water over the water-soluble ink, including the canal. Brush colour over the doors, darkening them with more ink if necessary. Dilute some sepia ink (or use sepia watercolour paint) and brush it over the cast shadows on the building, keeping within the pencil marks.

10 Using a fine paintbrush and white gouache, paint in the reflections of the doors in the water. Gouache paint used straight from the tube can be quite thick so only dip the tip of your brush into it.

The finished drawing

This is an evocative and elegant pen-and-ink study of a classic Venetian building. Permanent ink was used for the linear details in the most important areas, while brushing water over the water-soluble ink has helped to create areas of tone that soften the harshness of the pen work, transforming an architectural study into something much more picturesque. Although only one colour of ink was used, a good range of tones was created by washing water over different densities of hatched marks.

Both permanent and water-soluble ink were used here, creating a combination of linear detail and soft tonal washes.

The linear detailing of the building, as in the balcony, was drawn using permanent ink.

White gouache paint, which is opaque, is used to paint the light reflections on top of the dark patches of water.

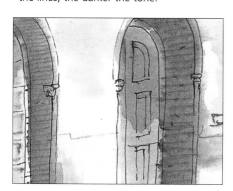

Washing water over hatched lines produces an area of solid tone – the closer together the lines, the darker the tone.

Cityscape

Although a construction site might not seem the most obvious choice of scene for a drawing project, if you choose your viewpoint carefully, the bold colours and graphic shapes can give you the chance to create a modern-looking, semi-abstract drawing. It will also test your ability to draw straight lines – always important when drawing buildings, whatever era they date from.

Scenes such as this can be found in towns and cities all over the world and recording a new building at all stages of its construction, from site clearance through to completion, makes an interesting long-term project. Moreover, many companies are waking up to the investment potential of buying original art – so who knows? If there's a prestigious building project going on near your home and your work is good enough, you might even be able to persuade them to buy it to display in the reception area or to use in promotional literature.

Oil pastels are not renowned for their subtlety of colour, but for a subject such as this, which relies on the bold, primary colours of the building cranes for much of its impact, they are ideal. You need to press quite firmly on the oil pastels, so use a heavy drawing paper or an oil-painting paper for this project to avoid the risk of tearing the support.

Materials
- *Heavy drawing paper or oil-painting paper*
- *4B pencil*
- *Oil pastels: pale greys (warm- and cool-toned), bright blue, red, yellow, white, lilac, Naples yellow, black*
- *Scraperboard tool or craft (utility) knife*

The scene
The brightly coloured cranes stand out dramatically against the cloudless blue sky, while the straight lines of the cranes and the buildings under construction create a graphic, almost abstract composition. The diagonal lines of some of the cranes make the composition more dynamic.

1 Using a soft pencil, mark out the lines of the cranes and the buildings under construction. There's no need to put in any of the internal lines at this stage, but do make sure you measure all the angles and distances carefully.

2 Using pale grey oil pastels, block in the building on the right. Note that the shaded sides are cooler in tone than those in full sunlight, so alternate between warm- and cool-toned greys as required.

4 Begin putting in the red lines of the cranes, using bold, confident strokes and pressing quite hard on the tip of the pastel. Lightly stroke the side of the pastel over the warm-toned shadow areas of the buildings.

3 Block in the sky, using the side of a bright blue oil pastel and making sure you don't go over the lines of the cranes. Putting in the negative shapes of the background sky at this early stage makes it easier to see any thin lines of the cranes that you have not yet drawn.

Tip: It's easy to lose track of where you are in a complicated drawing such as this, so refer continually to your reference photo to make sure you don't apply the sky colour over any of the lines of the cranes.

5 Now put in the bright yellow of the cranes, filling in the spaces between the rungs with blue. Work white oil pastel over part of the sky and blend it with your fingers.

6 Using the side of a lilac oil pastel, roughly block in the shaded sides of the buildings on the right. (Note, in particular, the shadow cast on the building on the far right of the image.) Apply the same colour to some of the shaded interior floors of the building on the left. Work Naples yellow, which is a pale, warm yellow, over the warm-toned area of the building in the centre and add small dashes of red on the tall foreground building.

7 Using the tip of a black oil pastel to make strong, bold marks, draw the reinforced steel joists of the building in the background. Establish the different storeys of the building on the left, using a range of shadow colours (blue, lilac, black) as appropriate. Use the side of the pastels to make broad, lightly textured marks; you can then go over them with other pastels to blend the colours optically and create a more interesting shadow colour.

▶

Assessment time

The drawing is nearing completion and only a few minor adjustments are needed. In places, the cranes are lost against the building or the sky and need to be more sharply defined. Some of the shadows need to be darkened slightly.

This crane merges into the building behind it and needs to be a little more clearly defined.

The lines of the white crane are quite delicate and will be hard to draw with a thick oil pastel.

8 Using a scraperboard tool or the tip of a craft knife, scratch off blue oil pastel to create the lines of the white crane in the centre of the image.

9 Scratch into the red crane on the left to create some highlight areas, and strengthen the red diagonal line so that the crane really stands out against the building.

The finished drawing

This artist has matched the medium to the subject beautifully. The bold, vibrant colours of oil pastels, which might be too brash and unsubtle for many subjects, are perfect for the bright, primary colours of the cranes and sky. Although it is difficult to draw fine details with oil pastels, they are the ideal drawing tool for the solid, graphic lines of this scene. Using the side of the pastels for the façades of the buildings brings another quality to the image and creates a lighter texture. Overlaying one colour on another, particularly in the shadow areas, has created interesting optical colour mixes that are much more lively and interesting than a flat application of a single colour could ever be.

Optical colour mixes create lively shadow colours.

The sgraffito technique allows you to scratch off the pastel and create fine lines.

Finger blending in the sky softens both the colour and the texture.

Sunshine and shadow

When you're drawing buildings, you can opt either for a very detailed approach that captures every single element, rather like an architectural drawing, or for something more atmospheric, as here, where the effects of light and shade are as important a part of the image as the buildings themselves.

In this project, the light is very strong and is illuminating the front of the buildings. If the light were coming from the side, the differences in tone between the shaded and brightly lit areas would be more pronounced. Nonetheless, there are still areas of deep shadow within the scene, particularly around the arched doorway – and it is these shadows that give depth to the façade. There is also a large shadow on the left of the scene, cast by a building behind the artist's viewpoint. This shadow occupies almost one-quarter of the drawing. Although it is dark, some detail is still visible within it so don't allow it to dominate the image completely.

Creating a strong enough contrast between very bright and very dark areas is the key to this drawing. As this is a charcoal drawing, the white of the paper is left untouched for the brightest areas. You can't make the light areas any lighter than they already are so, in order for the brightest areas to look really bright, you need to make the dark areas really dark.

Because the light on the brightest parts of the buildings is so strong, much of the detail is subdued. In many ways this is a bonus: when you're drawing a complicated subject like this, it's very easy to get obsessed with detail and put in so much that it detracts from the essential elements of the scene – the lively interplay between light and shade.

Materials
- *Smooth, heavy drawing paper*
- *Thin willow charcoal stick*
- *Clean rag or kitchen paper*
- *Kneaded eraser*

The scene
There is an interesting balance between light and dark in this scene, with the top of the buildings bathed in sunlight and the bottom half deep in shadow.

1 Using a thin charcoal stick, map out the shapes and proportions of the buildings, checking your measurements as you work. Use line only: there is no point in putting in any shading until the basic structure has been established.

2 Block in the dark recesses of the windows and the arched main door. Using the side of the charcoal stick, block in the shadow on the left-hand side, which is cast by a building behind the artist.

3 Using the tip of the charcoal, lightly block in the windows on the left-hand building. At this stage you are still establishing the basic shapes of the different architectural elements; refining the dark and light areas will come later. Smooth out the cast shadow with your fingertips.

4 Begin to put more detail on the buildings, such as the windows above the arched doorway and the rose window on the front façade. The windows above the arch are among the darkest areas, so you can afford to press quite hard on the charcoal as you block in the shapes of these elements.

5 Continue adding dark details to the buildings. Using the side of the charcoal stick to get a broad, even coverage, darken the shadows at the base of the image and in the archway, and then gently smooth out the charcoal with your fingertips.

6 Lightly sweep the side of the charcoal stick over the sky area. Using a clean rag or a piece of kitchen paper and a gentle circular motion, smooth out the charcoal to give a soft tone. Note how the brightest parts of the right-hand building are beginning to stand out against the darkened sky.

▶

Assessment time

This is the time to stand back and assess the tonal values, as the drawing depends for its success on there being sufficient contrast between the very dark and the very light areas. You can't make the lightest areas any lighter, because the white of the paper is as light as you can get – so the only way to make the light areas really stand out is to darken the darks.

The shadows on the building look too light and hazy.

The lightest parts of the buildings are almost lost against the sky.

7 It's almost inevitable that you will have muddied the edges of the buildings when putting in the sky so, using a kneaded eraser, gently wipe around the edges of the buildings to give them a sharp outline. If your eraser is worn, shape a section with your fingertips to create a clean, sharp edge.

8 Adjust the tones across the image, darkening the sky slightly if necessary so that the buildings stand out more. The shadows in the bottom left need to be really dark, too. Draw the lamppost in the foreground, making it very dark so that it comes forwards in the image.

9 Continue refining the lights and darks across the whole image, and use the kneaded eraser to accentuate highlights and sharpen edges. The adjustments are minor at this stage, but you need to keep assessing the tonal values of the drawing overall.

The finished drawing

This is an atmospheric drawing that captures the fleeting effects of light and shade extremely well. The contrast between the solidity of the buildings and the smoothed-out, insubstantial-looking shadow areas is particularly effective. The artist has used the white of the paper to good effect for the brightly lit parts of the buildings; they are almost dazzlingly bright when compared with the deep shadows in the bottom left of the image. Although much of the detail is subdued because of the lighting conditions, we can see enough to know how grand and imposing the buildings are.

Smoothing out the shadow areas makes them appear less solid.

The lamppost is very dark, which brings it forwards in the image.

There is just enough tone in the sky to allow the brightly lit buildings to stand out.

Quick sketches of animals: Cows in a field

Of all the domesticated animals that one could draw, cows are probably the most docile – and, particularly when there's a plentiful supply of fodder, the most likely to stay in the same place for a reasonable amount of time. With luck, therefore, you may have time to work up a reasonably detailed sketch before they amble off to pastures new.

When you're drawing any group, be it a group of animals, people, or objects in a still life, you need to observe the spatial relationships between the different elements very carefully. Use grid lines (real or imaginary) to work out where things should be positioned, and remember to look at the negative shapes (the spaces between different elements), both to get the shapes right and to make sure that your composition is balanced.

One of the difficulties of working on location is that the light can change dramatically in the course of a few hours, so it's a good idea to make a note of the direction from which the light is coming. In the ten-minute sketch (below), the artist drew a small arrow to remind herself of the direction and angle of the sun.

The scene
Within a large group such as this, there are a number of potential scenes to draw. Rather than drawing the whole scene, try isolating different elements, as the artist has done in the sketches shown here, to find a grouping that you like. Remember that you may have to reposition other elements, such as the fence posts, in order to get the composition to work.

5-minute sketch: graphite and pastel pencils
Look for elements within the scene that you can use to help yourself position things. Here, the line of the barbed wire fence is a useful guide: the top wire is level with the eyes of the cow on the left while the bottom wire is level with the nose of the cow on the right. Even in just a few minutes, you can apply some colour to the basic shapes – either as a colour note to refer to later or simply to block in areas of dark tone.

10-minute sketch: graphite and pastel pencils
When you draw a line across the rumps of the two foreground cows, you can see that it runs parallel to the back of the cow in the background. (Guidelines would be rubbed out but have been left in here to show what was done.) Also, if you look down from the tip of the right-hand cow's left ear, you will see that it's level with the animal's left foreleg: by drawing in a faint line, you can place the leg accurately.

15-minute sketch: graphite and pastel pencils

Even though the cows' bodies are a single colour, look for differences in tone that will tell us about the form of the animal. In this scene, the sun is quite high in the sky and is hitting the animals' backs. By blocking in the tops of the backs in a lighter tone than the flanks, the artist has created some modelling that conveys the rounded shape of the cows' bellies.

20-minute sketch: graphite and pastel pencils

Building on the previous three sketches, this sketch conveys more of the texture of the animals' coats. Vigorous scribbles of pastel pencil hint at the semi-rough texture and indicate the direction in which the hairs grow.

Quick sketches of animals: Leopard

Whatever your views on the morality of keeping animals in zoos, they certainly give you the opportunity to study at first hand animals that are extremely difficult to get close to in the wild. Just like domestic cats, big cats spend a lot of their time drowsing or sleeping, which is the perfect time to sketch them. Even in this situation, however, you need to convey a sense of their strength and power – so think about the skeleton underneath the fur and about where the largest muscle groups are situated. And as in any portrait, human or animal, the eyes are vital in conveying the character.

When you are drawing fur or hair, always look at the direction in which it grows and make sure your pen or pencil marks run in the same direction. Think about the quality of the fur and alter your marks accordingly: are the hairs small and tightly compacted, as on the top of the animal's head, or longer and farther apart, as around the bridge of the nose? Remember that you do not need to put in every single hair: a suggestion is enough, as the viewer's brain will fill in the missing details.

10-minute sketch: soft pastels

Soft pastels are a wonderful medium for portraying the beautiful markings and the soft texture of the fur, as you can overlay one colour on top of another and blend the marks with your fingertips to create subtle optical mixes, while also putting down stronger marks for the dark spots. If you are pushed for time, try sketching just part of the face as a practice exercise, as the artist did here. Note how including just one eye immediately brings the 'portrait' to life.

The 'relaxed pose'

This apparently relaxed pose, with the leopard draped over the branch of a tree from where it can survey its surroundings, is characteristic of this large cat – and there's no mistaking the alertness in the eyes or the power of those huge neck muscles and jaws.

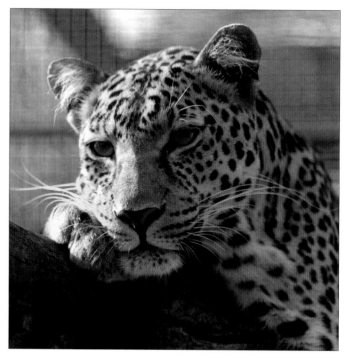

15-minute sketch: pen and ink

This is an exercise in creating the texture of fur using the harsh, linear medium of pen and ink. The sketch is incomplete, which is fine for a quick practice exercise in which you want to concentrate on just one aspect – but note how the artist has put in faint pencil guidelines marking the position and shape of the eyes. Getting the eyes right is critical in any portrait, human or animal.

30-minute sketch: charcoal

Like soft pastels, the powdery medium of charcoal is perfect for rendering the texture of fur. Here, the artist worked on a pale but warm-toned grey pastel paper, so that she could start from a mid-tone. A brilliant white paper would have been too stark and unsympathetic. Note how she has captured the shape and form of the animal's skull through her use of shading: the left-hand side of the head and what we can see of the body are in shade, while the left eye is more deeply recessed still. As in the pastel drawing opposite, the artist has blended the charcoal marks with her finger or a torchon to create the softness of the fur, while adding dark scribbles on top for the actual markings.

Quick sketches of animals: Short fur

This breed of dog has relatively short fur, which means that the muscles and bone structure are more obvious than in long-haired species. But the fur is also quite thick and you need to convey a sense of this in your drawing. The best way to achieve this is to build up the texture gradually, using light, short pencil or pen strokes until you have the desired effect.

As for colour and tone, even areas that, on first glance, appear to be pure white or a solid black will contain other tones. Observe this carefully: the fur follows the contours of the animal, so capturing changes in tone will help you to convey the shape of the animal, be it a stocky body, as here, or the streamlined silhouette of a greyhound.

Start from the eyes because once you have placed the eyes, it is easier to map out the rest of the head and its features. When you have completed the head, you can use it as a guide to work out how big the body is in relation to the head.

The 'pose'

This alert stance, with head and tail erect and feet planted squarely on the ground, is typical of the breed. The side-on viewpoint gives you the opportunity to study both the anatomy of the animal and the markings and texture of the fur, while the lolling red tongue adds a splash of colour to an otherwise muted range of browns and blacks.

5-minute sketch: B pencil

Even in a very short space of time, you can put down the essentials of the animal's 'pose'. Look at the dog's stance: here the legs are planted four square on the ground, but in a moving animal the balance would be very different. Measure the size of the head and legs in relation to the body and roughly scribble in the darkest patches of fur to give some indication of the position of the markings.

15-minute sketch: coloured pencils

Here, the artist has added more texture and detailing to the animal's fur (as well as adding colour to the dog's tongue). Note the short, jagged strokes around the edges, rather than a smooth outline, and how the pencil marks follow the direction in which the fur grows. A range of browns was used in this sketch, starting with the lightest and moving on to the darkest in order to build up the colours and tones gradually.

30-minute sketch: black ballpoint pen

Even with an ordinary ballpoint pen, which does not allow you to vary the width of the line that you produce, it's amazing how much variety of tone you can achieve if you take the time and trouble to build up the drawing gradually. Note how much more textured the fur is in this sketch than in the ones on the opposite page. It also has depth: light marks in the brightest areas (on the dog's shoulder, for example) indicate the shadows within the fur and tell us that the individual hairs are relatively short.

Tips: When drawing fur, make sure that your pencil or pen marks follow the direction in which the fur grows.

• Remember that fur rarely, if ever, lies completely flat: use sharp, spiky marks around the edge of the animal's body to convey the texture and length of the fur.

• Within areas that appear at first glance to be a single tone, look for subtle differences that will help you to convey the underlying shape of the animal and the direction of the light.

Old English Sheepdog

The breed of Old English Sheepdogs are delightful and their faces (or the little that you can see underneath the animal's shaggy hair) are full of character. A textural study seems particularly appropriate for this breed, whose whole character is defined by its long, flowing fur. For a short-haired breed such as a Whippet or a Great Dane, a more linear drawing that emphasizes the muscles might be more suitable.

When you're drawing long-haired animals such as this, however, it's very easy to be seduced into concentrating on the wispy, flyaway fur and to forget about the bone structure of the animal underneath. Always start by establishing the underlying structure, and then add the decorative and textural detail on top. The way to do this is to start by drawing prominent features such as the eyes, nose, mouth and any bony protuberances near the surface. Once you've got their shape, size and position right, the rest will follow much more easily.

When drawing any kind of portrait, be it human or animal, it is a good idea to begin by positioning the facial features. Think of the eyes and nose as an inverted triangle: establish the outer point of each, as this will make it easier to get the rest of the features in the right place. If you start by drawing the outline of the head, you may find that you haven't left enough space to fit in the features.

In a monochrome drawing, you also have to think carefully about tone. Monochrome might seem ideal for an animal whose coat consists almost entirely of white and grey tones, but a very common beginner's mistake is to make the greys too light: consequently, the whole image can appear to be lacking in contrast. Reassess the tones continually, and be prepared to adjust them as you work and to darken the darks in order for the light tones to sparkle and shine through.

Materials
• *Smooth drawing paper*
• *Graphite pencils: HB, 6B*
• *Torchon*
• *Plastic eraser*

The subject
When you're drawing an animal (or a person, for that matter) always look for a characteristic pose or expression. The lolling pink tongue is typical of this breed of dog and gives the animal a quizzical, slightly comical expression that is very appealing. You can't rely on animals to stay still for long, however, so (unless you're an experienced artist and can draw quickly) you'll probably find it easiest to work from a reference photograph.

1 Using an HB pencil, lightly sketch your subject. Start with the facial features, as once you get these right, the rest will follow relatively easily. Note that the eyes and nose form an inverted triangle and begin by putting down the outer points of each as a guide. Roughly shade the eyes, nose and tongue, and indicate the direction in which the fur grows around the head.

2 Using a 6B pencil, darken the nose and the sockets of the eyes. Note that, because the dog's head is turned ever so slightly to one side, one eye appears to be fractionally larger than the other. Use a torchon to blend the graphite on the nose and tongue to get a smooth, soft coverage. Also use the torchon as a drawing tool to apply some tone to the fur around the nose.

3 Again using the 6B pencil, draw the mouth (which can just be glimpsed around the tongue) more clearly. As in the previous step, use the torchon as a drawing tool to apply some tone to the fur on the dog's face and body. Your strokes should follow the direction in which the fur grows.

4 Loosely define the outer limits of the fur around the head to give yourself a boundary towards which to work. Using a 6B pencil, put in the darkest areas of fur on the dog's face, always making sure your pencil strokes follow the direction in which the fur grows.

6 Using the edge of a plastic eraser, wipe off fine lines of graphite to create the white hairs around the eyes. (It is easier to wipe off white details than to apply dark tones around them.)

5 Blend the graphite marks with a torchon to create smooth areas of tone between the eyes and on the face.

7 Using an HB pencil, draw more mid-toned hairs around the mouth. Wipe the eraser across the dog's face above the mouth to create the lighter-toned fur in this part of the face.

▶

Assessment time

The sheepdog's eyes, nose and mouth areas are prominent points that establish the structure of the dog's skull; the surrounding shaggy fur, by comparison, can be regarded as little more than decorative detail. For the rest of the drawing, concentrate on looking at the tones within the fur. Your shading in this area will convey the colour of the fur and also, because of the way the fur falls, imply the bony structure of the skull underneath.

It's hard to tell where the head ends and the body begins. One of your next tasks will be to delineate this more clearly.

More detail and texture is needed on the face.

8 Now you can complete the textural detail of the fur. Using an HB pencil with a fine point, draw more individual wispy hairs – particularly around the nose and eyes. Beware of applying too much detail to the body; this would detract from the head, which is the most important part of the drawing.

9 Using a 6B pencil, reinforce the dark line on the left-hand side to try to make it clearer where the head ends. Assess the drawing as a whole and readjust tones by blending graphite with a torchon or lifting out tone with an eraser wherever you judge it to be necessary.

The finished drawing

This is a charming study of a well-loved family pet, and an interesting exercise in texture. The texture of the fur is created through a combination of softly blended pencil marks and more linear strokes for individual hairs on the face. The fact that the dog is looking directly at us immediately engages us in the portrait.

The eye socket has depth; it appears as a rounded form rather than a flat circle on the surface of the face.

The texture of the fur is created through a combination of marks blended with a torchon and individual linear strokes.

The dark line of the lower lip helps to make the lolling tongue stand out more clearly in the drawing.

Short-eared Owl

Feathers and fur make wonderful subjects for a drawing. You don't even need to draw the whole animal: close-up details concentrating on the wonderful colours and patterns can make very striking semi-abstract works of art.

This drawing is made using coloured pencils, the fine tips of which enable you to capture the subtle coloration to perfection. Although on first glance it looks as if the bird is predominantly white and brown, there are many different colours within the dark areas – blue-greys and blacks as well as a range of browns. Paying attention to these differences will give your drawing depth and form, as they reveal the shaded areas within the feathers. Beware of using pure black for the very darkest areas, however: it's a very harsh, unforgiving colour and a combination of indigo and a very dark brown will give you a softer, more sympathetic result.

Take plenty of time to build up the texture. Get it right and you'll almost feel as if you could ruffle the feathers with your fingertips. Use short pencil strokes that follow the direction in which the feathers grow. The highlights are not very obvious in the reference photo, so you need to work out where they would appear: as any light source is likely to be above the subject, they are normally in the upper part of the eye. Note also that the owl's head is turned slightly to one side, so we can see more of one eye than the other.

The most important thing in a drawing like this is to keep referring to your reference photo to ascertain the lights and darks. Stand back from your drawing at regular intervals and assess it as a whole. It's easy to get caught up in detail and concentrate on the tip of your pencil rather than on the overall effect.

Materials
- *Smooth, heavy drawing paper*
- *2B pencil*
- *Coloured pencils: primrose yellow, olive green, gold or mid-yellow, gunmetal or charcoal grey, blue-grey, indigo, chocolate brown, sepia,*
- *Tracing paper*
- *Pencil sharpener*
- *Kneaded eraser*

The subject
You'd have to be very lucky to get so close to such a magnificent bird in the wild. This owl was photographed at an owl sanctuary. Whatever you think about zoos and wildlife parks, they do provide an opportunity to admire and draw specimens that might otherwise be difficult to see.

1 Using a 2B pencil, lightly sketch the subject. Map out the blocks of dark-coloured feathers across the bird's head and body with light, gentle strokes.

2 Using a primrose yellow pencil, colour in the iris of the eye and put tiny strokes of olive green over the darkest part (the part immediately below the pupil) to darken the yellow. Go over the iris again with gold or a mid-yellow pencil.

3 Colour in the pupils of the eyes, using a gunmetal or charcoal grey pencil and leaving a highlight in each pupil untouched. Go over the pupil again with a blue-grey pencil. Using an indigo pencil, put down the first indication of the feathers that grow around the eyes.

4 Go over the pupil again with indigo and the iris with mid-yellow. Note how these successive layers build up, creating a smooth, almost glossy surface colour. Outline the eyes with an indigo pencil and put in some of the feather detail around the eyes with the same colour.

5 Put in the beak with a blue-grey pencil, leaving the bright highlight untouched. Go over the darkest part with a chocolate brown pencil. Use tiny pencil strokes for the feathers that overlap the top of the beak. Take care not to make the beak too dark or it will overpower the whole image.

6 Using a sepia pencil, put in the dark feathers on the owl's face and head. Use little, jagged scribbling strokes that follow the direction in which the feathers grow so that you begin to get some realistic-looking texture into the feathers. Look at the relative length of the feathers, too: those around the ears are longer, so make long pencil strokes, using the side of the pencil rather than the tip.

Tip: The pencil point will wear down very quickly. Roll it around in your fingers as you work, so that it doesn't blunt into a wedge shape. Sharpen all your pencils regularly.

7 At this point you need to define the outline of the bird without creating a rigid line. Use short, wispy, horizontal strokes around the edge of the face and vertical strokes for the body behind, as the difference in direction helps to define the form, and leave some gaps around the outline for the white feathers. Continue mapping out the dark areas of feathers on the face, using blue-grey and sepia pencils as before.

▶

8 Continue working around the top of the head, using jagged, scribbling strokes as in Step 6 and alternating between charcoal grey and sepia pencils as appropriate. For the very darkest feathers, use chocolate brown. This immediately gives the feathers more depth and we can begin to see the different layers.

9 Darken the side of the face with sharp, jagged strokes of indigo, so that it stands out more clearly from the body. Some areas within the face are still completely empty of pencil marks. Using the side of the pencil, make light strokes for the feathers in this area. Although the feathers are largely white, you need to introduce some tones of pale grey here as there are shadows within them.

10 Build up the colours on the owl's face using the same pencils as before – indigo and chocolate brown for the very darkest areas, and blue-grey and charcoal grey elsewhere. The area around the eyes is particularly important: build up the dark feathers here so that you see the eyeball as a rounded form rather than as a flat circle on the surface of the face. Begin mapping out the darkest blocks of feathers on the body, using the side of a chocolate brown pencil. The feathers are bigger here than on the face, so you can be less precise about their placement and shape.

Assessment time
The drawing is progressing well, but more detailing is needed on the side of the head and the body. Work slowly and deliberately: it is amazing how much texture you can create by building up the layers of pencil work.

Our attention is drawn to the eyes, but the vivid yellow needs to be still more vibrant.

The face is in danger of merging into the body and needs to stand out more clearly.

Only the main blocks of feathers have been put in on the body. More detail and texture are required.

11 Go over the irises again with another layer of primrose yellow and olive green to intensify the colour and create a smooth, glossy surface that contrasts well with the soft ruffles of the feathers. Reinforce the dark feathers on the owl's face with indigo and chocolate brown. Repeat the process on the body, using the side of the pencil rather than the tip to create broader marks. (The clumps of feathers are larger here, so you can be less precise with your marks.)

12 Darken the beak with indigo, so that it stands out from the feathers, taking care not to obliterate the highlights. Use long, smooth pencil strokes to create the hard, bony texture. Reassess the feathers on the face, and add more definition if necessary.

The finished drawing

This drawing is a perfect demonstration of how successive layers of coloured pencil marks can create detailed textures and depth of colour. The key is patience: if you rush a drawing like this, you will not achieve such subtlety and detailing. Contrasts of texture – the hard, shiny beak versus the soft, ruffled feathers and the shiny, moist eyes – are vital.

Note the intensity of colour created by gradually building up successive layers of different colours.

The highlight on the beak helps to indicate its curving shape, hard, bony texture and slightly shiny surface.

The face stands out well from the body, thanks to the jagged pencil marks used for the feathers in this area.

Chickens

When you're drawing birds, you can opt either for a very detailed and painstaking rendition of the feathers or for a more impressionistic approach that attempts to recreate the lovely sheen. This project takes the latter route and relies on a combination of building up layers of water-soluble oil pastel to give a rich sheen and making linear, textural marks with both oil pastel and water-soluble pencil.

The project also involves brushing water over the pigment in order to blend it on the support and create the right colour mixes – so use a medium-weight or heavy watercolour paper which will be absorbent enough for you to be able to apply water without it cockling. Work with your drawing board flat for these stages, so that the colour doesn't run where you don't want it to go.

Look carefully and you will see that, even in areas that at first glance appear to be a single colour, there are many different colours within the birds' feathers – rich browns, oranges and yellows, with blues and violets in the darkest, most shaded parts. The feathers also have a slight iridescence, which is very hard to convey accurately. However, applying layers of colour on top of one another creates lively optical colour mixes that give something of the effect.

Materials

- *Watercolour paper*
- *Water-soluble pencils: grey, dark brown*
- *Ruling drawing pen*
- *Masking fluid*
- *Water-soluble oil pastels: dark olive green, yellow ochre, grass green, pinkish brown, bright yellow, orange, burnt sienna, violet, bright green, red, blue, brown*
- *Brush*
- *Kitchen paper*

The scene

This artist spotted these two chickens in a local farmyard and was attracted by the colourful plumage and lovely rounded shapes. She had to take a reference photo quickly, since the chicken on the left was about to walk away. She decided to swap the birds around in her drawing so that they would be facing one another, as this made a more pleasing composition.

1 Lightly sketch the scene using a grey water-soluble pencil. To give yourself a guide when you apply the colour, draw some light lines within the outline of the birds to indicate the positions of the main blocks of feathers, such as the wings.

2 Using a ruling drawing pen, apply masking fluid over the lightest parts of the image, where you want to preserve the white of the paper – the white feathers, the chickens' legs and the tall stems of grass in the foreground.

4 Scribble yellow ochre and dark olive green oil pastel over the foreground, adding pinkish brown oil pastel where the dry, dusty earth can be seen under the grass stems.

3 Loosely scribble dark olive green water-soluble oil pastel over the background, working around the chickens. Work some yellow ochre and grass green oil pastel over the top.

Tip: You need to press quite hard on the oil pastels, so take care not to dislodge the masking fluid.

5 Brush clean water lightly over the foreground and background, blending the colours on the support and making sure that no colour spills over on to the chickens.

6 Now you can begin applying colour to the chickens. Work bright yellow water-soluble oil pastel around the neck and tail feathers, making vertical marks that follow the direction in which the feathers grow. Overlay orange oil pastel for the darkest orange parts. Use burnt sienna for the dark browns and add violet for the very darkest parts so that you begin to develop a sense of the depth of the feathers.

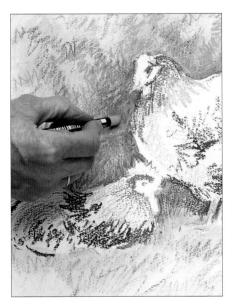

7 Darken the background behind the birds so that they stand out more, making jagged strokes of bright green to give a grass-like texture.

8 Carefully brush clean water over the birds. Keep a piece of absorbent kitchen paper to hand to dab off any excess water so that you can control where the colour goes.

Tip: Rinse your brush frequently so that you don't contaminate the light orange areas with dark violet or brown.

9 Put in the red combs, using both red and orange water-soluble oil pastels to get the right shade of orangey-red. Wash over with clean water to blend. Dip the tip of a dark brown water-soluble pencil in water and, using short feathery strokes, draw in the ruffle at the base of the neck and the large feathers that lie around the base of the wing. (Dipping the pencil in water intensifies the colour, while the linear pencil strokes add texture.)

Assessment time
The drawing is nearing completion and contains an interesting mix of linear marks, which create texture in the grass, and softly blended colour. However, more detail is needed on the chickens' feathers, both to add texture and to increase the depth of colour and create a realistic-looking sheen.

The grass in the foreground needs more colour and texture, as this will help to imply that it is closer to the viewer.

Although this area is the most brightly lit part of the chicken, it looks too stark at present; it needs more texture and detail.

10 Gently rub over the drawing with your fingertips to remove the masking fluid that you applied in Step 2. Using the dark brown water-soluble pencil, put more detail into the feathers, as in Step 9. Scribble blue oil pastel into the darkest parts of the feathers. Darken the birds' upper bodies by applying short, linear marks with a brown oil pastel.

11 If any of the highlights look too big or bright now that you've removed the masking fluid, dot in any appropriate feather colours to subdue them and make them less obtrusive. Add any final linear detailing on the feathers, using the same colours as before in either oil pastel (for thicker marks) or water-soluble pencil (for fine lines).

The finished drawing

This is a colourful and lively drawing that demonstrates that you don't need to put in every minute detail to achieve a realistic-looking image. The artist has exploited the soft, buttery consistency of the water-soluble oil pastels to create blended layers that convey the sheen on the feathers, while linear marks made using both the oil pastels and water-soluble pencils convey the texture of both the feathers and the grasses.

Masking fluid preserves the highlights on the feathers, allowing you to work freely without fear of covering them up.

Linear marks overlaid on blended areas of water-soluble oil pastel create the texture of the grasses.

The waxy consistency of the oil pastels helps to create a rich, glossy sheen on the birds' feathers.

Swimming fishes

This colourful project combines elements of both drawing and painting. In the early stages, water-soluble pencils are used in a linear fashion as drawing tools; later, they are washed over with clean water, so that the pigment spreads on the support just like watercolour paint. You can also apply dry water-soluble pencil over wet washes to deepen the colour, either by using the pencils directly or by brushing water over the tip of the pencil so that the brush picks up a little pigment. The benefit of this technique is that you don't create hard edges.

As you'll be applying water to the paper, use watercolour paper, which is absorbent enough not to tear under the weight of the water. When you start applying water, work on one part of the image at a time – first the fishes, then the water – so that the colours don't all blur together.

One of the most attractive aspects of this project is the sense of movement in the water. Observe how the ripples catch the light as this will help you to convey the movement. Use curved pencil strokes that follow the ripples and look at how the water breaks around the fishes.

Materials
- *Watercolour paper*
- *Water-soluble pencils: orange, bright yellow, dark blue, olive green, yellow ochre, warm brown, reddish brown, red, blue-green*
- *Masking fluid and old dip pen*
- *Paintbrush*
- *Kitchen paper*

The subject
The colouring on the fishes is spectacular – strong, saturated reds, yellows and oranges. Note how the shape of the fishes is slightly distorted by the ripples in the water. The ripples themselves catch the light from above, which creates a glorious sense of movement and shimmering light.

1 Using an orange water-soluble pencil, lightly sketch the outline of the fishes, making a clear distinction between the top of the larger fish's head, which is just poking out of the water, and the rest of the body. Draw a few of the largest ripples in the water, too.

2 Using masking fluid and an old dip pen, mask out the white highlights on the water and the fishes. Leave to dry.

Tip: You can speed up the drying process by using a hairdryer.

3 Lightly scribble bright yellow over all except the white parts of the fishes. Apply orange to the reddest areas, pressing quite hard on the pencil.

4 Now start putting some colour into the water, using dark blue with a few touches of olive green for the very darkest parts.

5 Colour in the submerged fins of the large fish using a yellow ochre pencil and go over the reddest part of both with a warm brown. Continue adding colour to the water, using the same colours as before and making curved strokes that follow the shape of the ripples.

Assessment time

You've now put down virtually all the linear detail that you need. Once you start applying water, however, there's a risk that you might lose some of the detail: it's important, for example, to retain some of the ripples in the water – so decide in advance where you want the pigment to spread and, if the colours run into areas where you don't want them to go, be ready to mop them up with a piece of absorbent kitchen paper.

Although the shape of the fish is clear, it's hard to tell which parts are submerged and which are above the water.

Confident, flowing linear marks capture the ripples in the water – and at least some of these marks should be visible in the finished drawing.

6 Dip a paintbrush in water and gently brush over the large fish. Note how intense and vibrant the colour becomes.

7 Brush clean water over the painted water, following the lines of the ripples and leaving some highlight ripples white.

 Tip: You may find it best to lay the drawing flat at this stage, so that the water doesn't run down it.

 Tip: If the water runs where you don't want it to go, simply blot it off with absorbent kitchen paper.

9 Dip a red pencil in water and darken the red of the fishes where necessary. Reinforce the outlines of the fishes with a blue pencil. Leave to dry.

8 Brush clean water over the small fish. Allow the support to dry slightly, but not completely, and go over the reddest parts of the fishes with a reddish brown pencil. The colour will intensify. It will also blur and spread, so you won't get any hard edges. The blurred orangey-red will look as if it is under water – so it will become clearer which parts of the large fish are jutting up above the water's surface.

10 Rub off the masking fluid. Scribble blue-green into the darkest parts of the water, pressing quite hard with the pencil to create the necessary depth of colour.

The finished drawing

This drawing demonstrates the potential and versatility of water-soluble pencils and combines linear detailing with lovely, fluid washes that intensify the colours and blend them together on the support.

Masking fluid can be used to keep the highlights white.

Curved pencil strokes create a sense of movement in the water.

The transition from one colour to the next is almost imperceptible.

Quick sketches of people: Artists at work

People who are engrossed in what they're doing make great subjects, as they'll probably be unaware that you're drawing them – a far less daunting prospect than asking someone to pose for you.

When you're drawing people, remember that the limbs are not separate entities: they're part of a linked, articulated skeleton. Even when your subjects are fully clothed, you must try to get a sense of the underlying structure and form of the body and of how the different parts interconnect. Creases in the fabric and distortions in any printed pattern on the cloth will give you clues about the shape of the body underneath.

When it comes to getting the proportions right, the only way to do it is to measure. You may have read that the head of an adult is equal to one-seventh of the total height. This is a generalization: the head is a useful unit to use to work out the height of the torso, but the proportions can vary considerably from one person to another – so always measure things for yourself.

The scene

These sketches (and on the next page) are of some of the artist's students hard at work in an outdoor painting class.

5-minute sketch: HB pencil

The artist here chose to draw just the outer two figures. You might be tempted to start by drawing the outlines of the figures, but you'll get a much better result if you think of the forms that lie under the hats and clothes. Lightly draw the whole oval of the skull, for example, and then superimpose the hat on top. Look at the tilt of the shoulders, the curve of the back and the angles at which the knees and arms are bent, as these will give you the dynamics of the pose. Loosely indicate which areas are in shadow.

10-minute sketch: HB pencil

In a slightly longer sketch (this time of the two right-hand figures), more detail is introduced, such as more precise shaping of the legs and an indication of where the sleeves and trouser legs end. You can take a bit longer to assess the shading so that the figures begin to look more rounded. It's often a good idea to make a monochrome sketch first, before you attempt to do the same thing in colour – otherwise you can find that you're distracted by the colours and don't properly assess how light or dark the tones need to be.

15-minute sketch: HB pencil, watercolour pencils and pen and ink
This sketch is a nice combination of pen-and-ink work for linear details, such as the lines of figures and the sketching stools, and coloured pencil for some simple patterning and shading on the clothes. Note the use of a cool blue for the areas of white clothing that are in shadow. The artist has also blocked in the background, allowing the figures to stand out more.

25-minute sketch: HB pencil, watercolour pencils and pen and ink
In 20 minutes or more, you have time to put more pattern on the clothes and to make the figures look rounded by indicating creases in the fabric of their clothes or through differences in tone. Here, the artist brushed over the water-soluble pencil work to create areas of soft tone.

Quick sketches of people: At the beach

The idea of sketching in public might seem rather daunting at first, but a beach or park is a great place to start. It's easy to find a quiet corner to hide away in – and there is usually so much going on that no one takes any notice anyway. In addition to drawing the whole scene, try pulling out individual figures from the crowd, too, for quick practice sketches. This is a great way of sharpening your observational skills.

When you are sketching people quickly, look for the essence of the 'pose' – the tilt of the head, the curve of the back, the angle of the shoulders. Remember this subtle but important clue to get a stance right: a movement in one part of the body is counter-balanced by a movement on the opposite side, in the opposite direction. So, if someone rests their weight on one leg, the opposite hip and shoulder will be thrust slightly upwards.

5-minute sketch: pencil

This is a preliminary compositional sketch for a painting. The curving path naturally leads our eye through the scene. The foreground umbrella and the lamp on the left balance each other; both are placed on the third, which is a strong position for features of interest in a drawing, and together they form a strong diagonal line across the composition.

The scene

This artist selected a viewpoint from the esplanade above the beach. Looking down on a crowded scene makes it much easier to separate the different elements from each other and to work out a pleasing composition. Drawing the same scene from beach level would have resulted in a confusing jumble of shapes and figures.

10-minute sketch: oil pastel

This sketch was made in oil pastels on beige-coloured pastel paper, which is similar to the colour of the sand. It imparts a warm mood to the image while a loose smear of blue hints at the sea beyond. Oil pastels are a handy tool for making quick sketches: although they're fairly chunky, which means you cannot make very fine, detailed sketches, they enable you to block in large areas quickly. Note how the artist has captured the young woman's stance with just a few swift marks: the brown marks laid over the pale blue of her T-shirt show how the fabric creases and give important information about her posture. The colour is smudged to create the shadows beneath the figures. The shadows give the image immediate depth and help to 'anchor' the figures.

25-minute sketch: pen and ink, wash

This sketch was made using a dip pen – which gives a fresh, spontaneous quality of line – and waterproof ink. Washes of dilute ink are used to create areas of tone, such as the shadow under the umbrella and the boat, the wedge-shaped wall on the left and the flesh tones. Note the different textures created by using different kinds of line: straight horizontal and vertical lines for the hard stonework and paving, small circles and squiggles for the soft sand.

Quick sketches of people: Al fresco lunch

Informal gatherings of family and friends are a great place to sketch people, as the atmosphere is relaxed and people behave naturally – but if you're nervous about sketching in front of other people, use the opportunity to take a few photos that you can use as reference material and then make your sketches later. With a large group, you may find that you need to direct the proceedings, in much the same way as a photographer at a wedding, in order to get the composition that you want. Don't feel intimidated about doing this – but remember that the people are there to enjoy themselves, not to pose for long periods of time while you try to capture their likeness on paper!

5-minute sketch: ballpoint pen
With a large group it can be hard to know where to start. Here the artist began by sketching the man in the hat, positioned just off centre, and then worked outwards in each direction. This helps to avoid the risk of making the first figure too big and running out of paper for the remaining figures.

The scene
Here, the artist selected his viewpoint carefully to create a balanced composition, with none of the heads overlapping. He felt that if everyone was looking directly at the camera the image would look too self-conscious and posed, so he asked the man and woman on the far left and right to look at each other, rather than at the camera. There is a good mix of full-face views (the three people at the back of the group), side profiles, and three-quarter views, giving you the chance to practise placing the facial features with the head turned at different angles.

15-minute sketch: pencil

Here, too, the artist began with the man in the hat. He then used the straight lines of the hat as a guide to help him assess the angles at which the sitters' heads were tilted. Light shading, done using the side of the pencil, introduces some tone into the image, while stronger crease lines in the clothing suggest the folds in the fabric and begin to give the image some form.

20-minute sketch: coloured pencils

This was made to provide the artist with rough colour notes that he could elaborate on later in a more detailed drawing. Note how the intensity of the blue in the men's shirts varies, with a deeper tone being used for the shaded creases. Even the white T-shirt of the man in the hat contains a surprising amount of blue, as his back is largely in shadow and there are many wrinkles in the fabric.

Male portrait

Drawing a portrait can be challenging but, as with all subjects, it helps if you can start by reducing things to basic shapes. Think of the face as an egg shape, with the wider end of the egg as the top of the head and the narrower end representing the chin.

The thing that beginners tend to find most difficult is placing the facial features accurately. Putting in a few guidelines – a central line through the forehead and down to the bottom of the chin, and lines across the face to mark the level of the eyes, nose and mouth – will help with this. As a general rule (although everyone is slightly different), the bottom of the eye socket is halfway down the face and the base of the nose is halfway between the eyes and the chin. The tops of the ears align with the eyebrows and the base of the ears with the base of the nose.

Remember that when the model's head is tilted slightly to one side, as here, you will be able to see more of one side of the face than the other – so the central line will not be centrally positioned. Moreover, as the head turns away, some features may overlap one another while others may be hidden from view altogether. In a three-quarters pose, for example, you will often find that the inner corner of the far eye is obscured by the top of the nose.

Rely on observation, not on your preconceptions about the relative sizes of features and where they sit in relation to one another.

Check your measurements, and then check them again, before you commit pencil to paper.

Materials

- *Drawing paper*
- *Thin charcoal stick*
- *Kneaded eraser*
- *Soft pastels: pewter grey, Naples yellow, dark brown, reddish brown, blue-grey, orangey brown, white*

The pose

This model has a strong profile, which the three-quarters pose (the head turned slightly to one side) shows off to advantage. As any portrait requires the same pose to be held for a long time, make sure your model is comfortable and, if he has to take a break, can resume the same position easily.

1 Using a thin charcoal stick, map out the head and shoulders. Think of the head as a three-dimensional geometric shape; all too often, beginners make the mistake of drawing a circular or oval outline for the face and forgetting that the head is a solid, three-dimensional form.

2 Draw a faint line down the centre of the face, from the top of the forehead to the chin. Then draw a line across the face to mark the level of the eyes. (Because of the tilt of the head, this line tilts up slightly here.) This line can also be used to indicate the level of the visible ear.

3 Establish the line of the nose, noting where it sits on either side of the central guideline, and the lips. You may find it helps to draw two inverted triangles – one from the outer edge of the eyes down to the tip of the nose and one from the outer edge of the eyes to the chin – as it is easier to judge positions within the triangles than by eye alone. Put in the eyes, remembering that the eyeballs must look rounded.

4 Now that you've established the positions of the features, you can erase your guidelines. Strengthen the line of the shoulders and the jaw. Using a pewter grey soft pastel, put in the eyebrows. Block in the lightest area of flesh tone – the cheek, the left of the forehead and the side of the neck – using the side of a Naples yellow pastel, which is a warm yellow well suited to this model's complexion.

5 Using the side of a pewter grey soft pastel, lightly put in the stubble and shadows on the face and around the inner edge of the shirt collar. Now put in some of the hair, using a very dark brown pastel. Look at how the hair grows over the skull and make your pastel strokes follow the direction in which the hair grows.

6 Continue working on the hair, noting that it grows in straight lines that go in different directions. Define the eyes more, noting how the lid wraps around the eye and preserving the catchlight – the lights reflected in the pupil. Using the pewter grey pastel again, introduce more tone on the shaded side of the face and in the hair.

▶

7 Use a dark reddish brown pastel to put in the lips. Use a thin charcoal stick to refine the shape of the nostril, the cleft in the chin and the overall line of the nose against the cheek. Using your fingertips, gently blend the grey charcoal on the areas of hair and stubble that are not quite as dark.

Assessment time
All the facial features are in place but more modelling is needed – particularly on the cheekbones as the shadows are not strong enough to reveal their form.

The hair is not dark enough and does not look shiny.

The cheekbones lack definition.

8 Roughly scribble in the hair, using a dark brown pastel. Remember to leave some areas lighter to show where the highlights fall and create a sheen on the hair. Lightly blend the marks with your fingertips, following the direction in which the hair grows.

9 Using a blue-grey pastel, hatch and blend the blue collar of the shirt. Use the same colour on the hair to give a slight blue-black sheen. Shape the nose, using an orangey brown pastel for the dark, shaded parts and the tip of a white pastel for the highlights.

The finished drawing

A strong profile is enhanced by the side lighting, which throws one side of the face into shadow. Although only a limited range of pastel colours was used, subtle blending captures the evenly coloured skin tones very well. The same technique creates the modelling on the face. Here, the artist chose not to colour in the model's sweater as she wanted to concentrate the viewer's attention on his face, but you could put in more colour if you wish.

Touches of blue-grey give the hair a smooth, glossy sheen.

Blended pastel marks create shadows on the cheeks and neck and under the chin.

Linear charcoal work is used to define the jawline.

Character portrait

Markets are a great place to make quick sketches or take snapshots of people going about their daily business, which you can then work up into more detailed portraits at a later date. People are so engrossed in what they're doing that they're unlikely to take much notice of you – so your photos and sketches may be much more informal and natural.

Here, the artist decided to omit both the background and the woman on the left and to concentrate on making a character portrait of the man – although you could, of course, include the setting, too, provided you keep the main emphasis of the drawing on his face.

This particular portrait gains much of its strength from the fact that there is direct eye contact between the subject and the artist, which immediately brings the portrait to life and makes the viewer feel involved in the scene. His gaze is quizzical, perhaps even slightly challenging, and even without the inclusion of the market setting, his slightly hunched pose and wrinkled face indicate that he leads a hard life.

Charcoal is a lovely medium for character portraits and, like black-and-white reportage or documentary-style photographs, a monochrome drawing has a strength and immediacy that works particularly well with this kind of subject. The same drawing in colour would have a very different feel – and probably far less impact. Why not try the same project in coloured pencil, too, to see the difference?

Materials
- *Fine pastel paper*
- *Thin charcoal stick*
- *Compressed charcoal stick*
- *Kneaded eraser*

The pose

In this scene two market traders in Turkey were spotted by chance rather than asked to pose formally. So these are character portraits. The artist concentrated on the man on the right, as the three-quarters pose, with direct eye contact, is more interesting than the head-on view of the lady. He has a strong profile, while the woman's face is more rounded and her features less clearly defined. The plastic sheeting could be confusing so it was omitted.

1 Using a thin stick of charcoal, map out the lines of the pose. Look at the angle of the shoulders and back and at where imaginary vertical lines intersect, so that you can place elements correctly in relation to one another. Here, for example, the peak of the man's cap is almost directly in line with his wrist.

2 Still using the thin charcoal stick, lightly put in guidelines to help you place the facial features. Draw a line through the forehead and down to the bottom of the chin, lines across the face to mark the level of the eyes, the base of the nose and the mouth, and an inverted triangle from the eyes down to the nose.

3 Refine the facial features and roughly block in the fur collar on the man's jacket. (It provides a dark frame for the face.)

4 Lightly draw the curve of the top of the skull. Although you can't actually see the skull beneath the cap, you can use the tilt of the head and the features you've already put in to work out where it should be. Remember that the base of the eye socket is generally about halfway down the face, so the top of the skull is likely to be higher than you might think.

5 Now you can draw the cap. Without the faint guideline of the skull that you drew in the previous step, you'd probably make the cap too flat and place it too low on the head. Draw the eyes and eyebrows and the sockets of the eyes. Already you can see how the form is beginning to develop.

▶

6 Sharpen the line of the far cheek and apply loose hatching on the far side of the face (which is in shadow) and on the forehead, where the cap casts a shadow.

Assessment time
The facial features are in place and most of the linear work has been completed, although the details need to be refined and the eyes darkened. Now you can begin to introduce some shading, which will make the figure look three-dimensional and bring the portrait to life.

The jacket looks flat. There is nothing to tell us how heavy it is or what kind of fabric it is made from.

Shading has introduced some modelling on the far side of the face, but more is needed.

7 Using a compressed charcoal stick, which is very dense and black, put in the line of the mouth.

8 Again using the compressed charcoal stick, put in the pupils of the eyes, remembering to leave tiny catchlights.

9 Using the side of a thin stick of charcoal, very lightly shade the right-hand side of the man's face. The shadow is not as deep here as on the far side of the face, but this slightly darker tone serves two purposes as it helps to show how tanned and weatherbeaten his face is and also creates some modelling on the cheeks.

10 Using the tip of your little finger, which is the driest part of your hand, carefully blend the charcoal on the right cheek to a smooth, mid-toned grey.

11 Using a kneaded eraser, pick out the highlighted wrinkles on the face, and the whites of the eyes.

 Tip: To get a fine point on the eraser for intricate areas, mould the eraser with your fingers.

12 Block in the dark, shaded side of the cap, using the side of the charcoal stick. Note that the cap is not a uniform shade of black all over: leave areas on the top untouched to show where the highlights fall.

▶

13 Using compressed charcoal, block in the fur collar on the jacket and smooth out the marks with your fingers. By making slightly jagged marks, you can suggest the texture of the fur. Note how the face immediately stands out more strongly when framed by the dark fur.

14 Put in the dark crease lines of the folds in the jacket. The deep creases help to show the weight of the fabric.

15 Using the side of the charcoal, apply tone over the jacket, leaving highlights on the sleeve untouched.

16 Using the side of your hand in a circular motion, blend the charcoal to a smooth, flat tone.

The finished drawing

This portrait is full of character. Note the classic composition, which draws our attention to the face. The overall shape of the portrait is triangular, with the strong line of the back leading up to the face and forming the first side of the triangle, and a straight line down from the peak of the cap to the arm forming the second side. In addition, the face is positioned roughly 'on the third' – a strong placement for the most important element in the drawing.

Wrinkles in the skin are picked out using the sharp edge of a kneaded eraser.

The crease lines and variations in tone show the weight and bulkiness of the fabric.

The direct eye contact between sitter and viewer makes this a very strong portrait.

Dancing couple

When drawing a moving subject, it's helpful to take a photograph to use as reference. You have two options. You can use a fast shutter speed to 'freeze' the action and risk losing the sense of movement that you wanted to capture. Alternatively, you can use a slower shutter speed so that there is some blur in the photo – but then you risk not being able to see all the detail as clearly as you would like. Here the artist wanted to see the detail clearly and elected to freeze the movement in the reference photo.

The challenge in this scenario is how to create that all-important sense of movement. Sometimes, even when the action is frozen, we know that the subject must be moving because the 'pose' itself is so precarious that we know it simply couldn't be held for more than a second or two. (Think, for example, of a ballerina in mid-pirouette.) Here the dancers have both feet touching the ground and the movement is not obvious at first glance, so you need to find other ways of conveying a sense of movement.

In this drawing the artist used two techniques to give a sense of movement: a 'ghost' image, indicating the position from which the limbs have just moved, and curved lines in the background, which follow the contours of the bodies. The same techniques could be applied just as well to other moving objects, for instance a horse racing at full stretch, a rally car speeding past on a country road, or any sporting action.

Manikin
Also called a lay figure, a manikin (available from art supply stores), is a very handy tool for working out the lines of a pose. Use it to help you to work out the 'ghost' image.

Materials
- *Pastel paper*
- *HB pencil*
- *Pastel pencils: brown, spectrum orange, black, light sepia, pale brown, red, orange, pale blue, cream or pale yellow, red-brown*

The pose
Although the action has been 'frozen' in this photo, the woman's flowing hair and the fact that the right foot of both dancers is in the process of lifting off the ground indicate that they are, in fact, moving.

1 Sketch the scene, using an HB pencil. Imagine guidelines running across and down the image to help you: the man's left hand, for example, is roughly in line with his right heel.

2 Block in the man's flesh tones and hair in brown and emphasize the strongest lines of the pose. Using spectrum orange, block in the woman's flesh tones.

3 Block in the hair of both dancers in black. For the shaded parts of the man's trousers and shirt and the woman's dress, apply light sepia. Use the same colour to draw the frill around the bottom of her dress.

4 Using the side of a pale brown pastel pencil, block in the background. Begin to put in stronger, curved lines in the background to emphasize the movement of the figures, echoing the curves of the moving arms.

▶

Assessment time

With the same pale brown pencil, put in a 'ghost' image of the moving legs and arms. This, along with the curved lines in the background which echo the shape of the woman's back, helps to give an impression of movement. Now that the main lines of the drawing have been established, you can begin to refine the detail and add some colour to bring the drawing to life.

The figures need to stand out more from the background.

5 Using the same colours as before, darken the flesh tones so that the figures stand out from the background. Block in the woman's dress and the man's waistcoat in red overlaid with orange. (This optical mix of two colours creates a much more lively and interesting effect than a solid application of a single colour.)

6 Using a very pale blue pencil, put in the creases in the man's shirtsleeve and shade his right leg. Block in the shoes in black, leaving the highlights. Working around the 'ghost' image, put in some stronger curved lines that follow the contours of the bodies to enhance the sense of movement.

7 Darken the creases on the trousers and go over the trousers very lightly with a cream or very pale yellow pastel pencil. (Leaving the paper white would look too stark.) Draw the woman's hair, which is streaming out behind her as she moves, with quick flicks of a black pastel pencil.

8 Using horizontal marks, put in the floor. It is on a different plane to the background and using horizontal, rather than vertical, strokes helps to make this clear. Using a red-brown pencil, sharpen the edges of the figures – the hands, faces, and the line of the woman's body and legs.

The finished drawing
The sense of movement in this drawing comes as much from the way the background has been handled as from the way the dancing couple has been drawn. The pastel pencil marks are light and free, which gives the drawing a feeling of energy.

The hair streams out, making it obvious that the dancers are moving quickly.

The 'ghost' images imply that this is the position the figure has just moved from.

Curved pencil strokes in the background also help to imply movement.

Male nude

People come in all kinds of shapes and sizes! Nonetheless, we can make some generalizations about the differences between men and women and you should bear these in mind when drawing a male nude. The main differences to note are that, generally, men have less fat tissue than women and look more angular. Men's shoulders are usually broader and their hips narrower. Typically, a man's neck looks shorter than a woman's and his feet and hands are larger in proportion with the rest of the body.

When making your initial sketch, it's tempting simply to outline the pose – but if you imagine the skeleton of the body underneath the skin as you draw, you will undoubtedly find it much easier to get the shapes right.

Materials
- *Grey pastel paper*
- *Thin willow charcoal stick*
- *Kneaded eraser*
- *Soft pastel: pale cream*

The pose
This sofa provides support, making the pose easy to hold for a long time. Even so, it's a good idea to mark the position of the feet and hands with pieces of masking tape, in case the model moves. The back is slightly bent and the stomach is convex, creating interesting shading on the torso. Note the slight foreshortening: the legs are closest to the viewer and so appear slightly larger than they would if the model were standing up.

1 Sketch the figure using a thin stick of charcoal, making sure you allow space for the sofa on either side. Measure and mark where each part of the body is positioned in relation to the rest; the face, for example, is in line with the model's left knee. Also look at the slope of the shoulders and at where the elbow is positioned in relation to the chest.

2 Begin searching out the form, making angular marks that establish the three-dimensional shape of the head and torso. Put in faint guidelines running vertically and horizontally through the centre of the face to help you position the facial features. Lightly mark the shape of the sofa – the curve of the arm and the cushion behind the model.

3 Once you've mapped out the basic composition, you can begin to strengthen the lines and put in the facial features in more detail. Draw the eyes, noting how the upper lids fold over the lower ones at the outer corners and how the line of the nose obscures the inner corner of the far eye. Roughly scribble in the hair line. Put in some shading under the chin, on the legs and arms, and on the left of the torso.

4 Using the tip of the charcoal, draw the muscle that runs diagonally along the side of the neck. This is a very strong, pronounced muscle and putting it in helps to emphasize the tilt of the head. Using the tip of your little finger, smooth out some of the shading on the torso and legs to create more subtle modelling. The figure is already beginning to look more three-dimensional.

5 Loosely scribble over the sofa, so that the figure stands out. Look at the negative shapes – the shape the sofa makes against the body – rather than at the body itself. This makes it easier to see if any adjustments need to be made to the outline of the body. Alter the direction of the hatching lines to make the different planes of the sofa more obvious.

6 Draw the model's left foot. (Try to think of it as a complete unit rather than a series of individual toes.) Shade one side, and indicate the spaces between the toes with very dark marks. Loosely scribble in the shadow cast on the base of the sofa by the model's legs, and hatch the different facets of the cushions.

▶

7 Use a kneaded eraser to gently clean up and create more contrast between the lightest and darkest parts. Darken the spaces between the fingers and indicate the segments of the fingers to show how they articulate.

Assessment time
Assess the tonal contrast of the figure as a whole to see where more shading or highlights are needed. For example, the lower part of the torso is slightly shaded by the ribcage as the model slumps back on the sofa, and this area needs to be darkened.

The upper part of the torso is a little too bright.

More shading is needed on the model's left leg.

8 Using a very pale cream pastel, put in the highlights on the face, right arm and leg. (Cream is a more sympathetic colour for flesh tones than a stark white.) Even though the limbs are rounded forms, the highlights help to define the different planes. Blend the pastel marks with your fingertip.

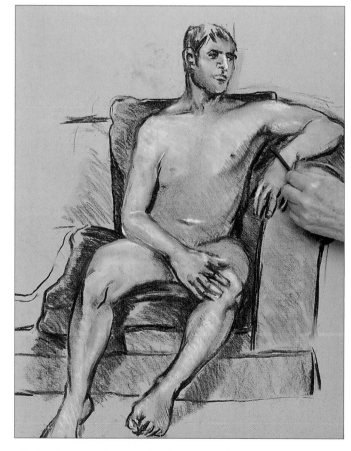

9 Apply more charcoal shading on the lower part of the torso, again blending the marks with your fingertip. (Use your little finger for blending, as it is the driest part of the hand and the risk of smudging the charcoal is reduced.) Darken the sofa under the model's arm, so that he stands out more.

The finished drawing
Although this is not an overly elaborate drawing, it conveys the muscular nature of the model's body. The calves and thighs, in particular, are well developed (this particular model is a professional dancer). Subtle shading reveals the different planes of the body and the combination of dark, intense charcoal marks and soft pastel works well.

Note how effectively shading conveys the muscles in the calf.

The pastel marks on the torso are blended to convey the smooth skin texture.

The figure stands out well against the dark background of the sofa.

Grandmother and young child

Family portraits, particularly of very young children, are always popular – and a project like this would make a wonderful present for a doting grandmother. Soft pastels capture the skin tones beautifully, and you can smooth out the marks with your fingers or a torchon to create almost imperceptible transitions from one tone to another. Build up the layers gradually. You can spray with fixative in the latter stages to avoid smudging the colours, but be aware that this may dull or darken the colours that you've already put down. Soft pastel is also a lovely medium for drawing hair, as you can put down many different colours within the hair mass to create depth and an attractive sheen. When drawing hair, look at the overall direction of the hair growth.

Young children have very short attention spans and they certainly can't hold the same pose for the time it takes to draw a detailed portrait. You'll be lucky if they sit still for long enough for you to do anything more than a very quick sketch – so working from a photograph is almost certainly your best option. Even then, it's very hard to get a young child to do exactly what you want. If you try to tell them what to do, the chances are you'll either get a very stilted shot, with the child staring grumpily at the camera, or he or she will wriggle and squirm, making an attractive shot virtually impossible.

One simple solution is to make the photo session into a game by pulling faces, clapping your hands, holding up a favourite toy and generally interacting with the child so that he or she forgets all about the camera. Above all, take lots of shots so you have plenty of reference material to choose from. Then you can combine material from several shots – invaluable if you can't get a shot in which both sitters are smiling at the same time.

Materials
- *Pale grey pastel paper*
- *Soft pastels: pinkish beige, white, dark brown, mid-brown, orangey beige, pale yellow, pinkish brown, reddish brown, dark blue, red, pale blue, grey, pale pink, black*

The pose
This is a happy pose, with both child and grandmother smiling broadly. To help them relax for the shot, the photographer got them to make a little game out of clapping their hands together which, in addition to helping them forget that they're having their photo taken, imparts a sense of movement to the pose.

1 Using a pinkish beige soft pastel map out the basic shapes – the heads of the two sitters and the position of the arms. Draw the sleeves and neckline of the grandmother's sweater in white pastel, putting in the most obvious creases in the fabric, and put in the slant of the little boy's shoulders in white, too.

2 Using the pinkish beige pastel again, indicate the position of the facial features by marking a central guideline with the eyes approximately halfway down. The grandmother's head is tilted back, so her eyes are a little above the halfway point. Roughly block in the child's hair and the shadows in the woman's hair in dark brown.

3 Still using the dark brown pastel, put in more of the hair, smudging the pastel marks with your fingers. Indicate the darkest parts of the facial features – the recesses of the eye sockets and nostrils. Apply some flesh tone to the child's face, using mid-brown for the darker parts and a more orange version of the beige used in Step 1 for the lighter parts. Using the side of a pale yellow pastel, roughly block in the base colour of the little boy's shirt.

4 Using the side of a white pastel, block in the grandmother's sweater. Apply a pinkish beige to her face and neck, blending the marks with your fingers.

5 The grandmother's neck is slightly warmer in tone than her face. Use a reddish brown for the slightly darker tones in this area, again blending the marks with your fingers. Use the same colour for the child's lips. Using your fingertips, smooth out the mid-brown on the child's face, leaving the orangey beige for the lighter parts. Use a very dark brown for the child's eyebrows and eyes.

6 Using a dark blue pastel, put in the creases in the fabric of the grandmother's sweater. Block in the arms, using a pinkish brown for the grandmother and a reddish brown for the little boy. Overlay various flesh tones – pinkish beige, orangey beige, red – as appropriate, blending the marks with your fingers. Flesh is not a uniform colour; look closely and you will see warm and cool tones within it.

7 With a dark brown pastel, put in the shadow under the child's chin and around the collar of his shirt. Put in some jagged strokes on the hair so that you begin to develop something of the spiky texture. Darken the child's eyes.

Tip: Think of the eyes as spherical forms rather than as flat circles on the surface of the face.

8 Using the same flesh colours as before, continue building up the modelling on the little boy's face. Add some red to the cheeks, blending the marks with your fingers. Like most toddlers, he has a fairly chubby face, so there are no deep recesses under the cheekbones, but with the mix of light and darker-coloured tones the flesh is starting to look more natural. Using the tip of a white pastel and dabbing on small marks, lightly draw his teeth and apply some tiny, glossy highlights to the lips.

9 Repeat the process of building up modelling on the grandmother's face. Apply pale yellow to her hair.

10 Continue working on the hair, putting in browns and greys to get some tonal variation within the hair. Note, too, how the hair casts a slight shadow on her face. Use a brown pastel to draw in the creases in the little boy's shirt. Draw in the crease lines around the grandmother's nose and mouth with a reddish brown pastel.

Assessment time

The expressions and pose have been nicely captured, but in places the skin tones appear as blocks of colour and need to be smoothed out more. A little more modelling is also needed on the faces and hands. The eyes need to sparkle in order for the portrait to come alive.

The pupils and irises have been carefully observed, but there is no catchlight to bring the eyes to life.

The child's hands, in particular, appear somewhat formless.

11 Continue the modelling on the grandmother's face and neck, gradually building up the layers and fleshing out the cheeks. Use the same colours and blending techniques as before. The adjustments are relatively minor at this stage.

12 Apply more yellow to the boy's shirt, scribbling it in around the dark crease marks. Smudge more brown over the yellow for the stripes in the fabric. A hint of the pattern is sufficient; too much detail would detract from the face.

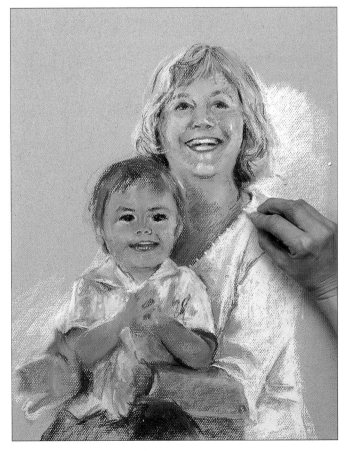

13 Using the side of the pastel, block in the grandmother's sweater with a very pale blue. Reinforce the dark blue applied in Step 6 to define the folds in the fabric. Apply tiny pale-blue dots around the neckline of the sweater.

14 Draw the little boy's fingernails with a pale pink pastel and apply light strokes of reddish brown between the fingers to separate them. Like his face, the fingers are fairly chubby so you don't need to put too much detail on them. Blend the marks with your fingertips if necessary to create soft transitions in the flesh tones.

15 If necessary, adjust the flesh tones on the boy's arms and fingers. Here, the artist judged that the face was too dark, so she applied some lighter flesh tones – a very pale orangey beige – to the highlights to redress the balance. Apply a range of browns to his hair to build up the texture and depth of colour.

16 Add a thin white line for the grandmother's necklace. Darken her lips and inner mouth; adjust the flesh tones. Redefine the creases around the nose and mouth if necessary.

17 The final stage is to put in some detail in the eyes – the black pupils and some tiny dots of white for the catchlights.

The finished drawing

This is a relaxed and informal portrait that captures the sitters' moods and personalities. Using soft pastel has allowed the artist to build up the flesh tones gradually, achieving a convincingly lifelike effect. Leaving the grandmother's hands slightly unfinished helps to create a sense of movement as she claps her hands together – in much the same way as a blurred photograph tells us that a subject is moving.

Leaving the hands unfinished creates a sense of movement.

The eyes sparkle: a tiny dot of white is sufficient to bring them alive.

Note how many different tones there are within the hair.

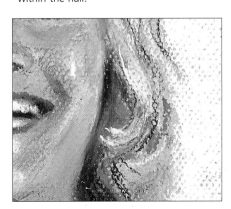

Glossary

Blending
Merging adjacent colours or tones so that they merge into one another. In dry, powdery drawing media, such as charcoal or soft pastel, blending is usually done with your fingers or with a torchon.

Charcoal
Charcoal is made by charring willow, beech or vine twigs at very high temperatures in an airtight kiln. It is available in powder form and as sticks. It can also be mixed with a binder and pressed into sticks ('compressed' charcoal), creating a form that is stronger than stick charcoal and does not break so easily. Charcoal pencils, made from compressed charcoal encased in wood, are also available.

Colour mixing
Optical colour mixing: applying one colour on top of another in such a way that both remain visible, although the appearance of each one is modified by the other. Also known as *broken colour*. Optical colour mixes tend to look more lively and interesting than their physical counterparts.

Physical colour mixing: blending two or more colours together to create another colour. Physical colour mixes tend to looks duller than their optical counterparts.

Cool colours
Colours that contain blue and lie in the green-violet half of the colour wheel. Cool colours appear to recede.

Composition
The way in which the elements of a drawing are arranged within the picture space.

Conté crayon
A drawing medium made from pigment and graphite bound with gum. Conté crayons are available as sticks and as pencils. They create an effect similar to charcoal but are harder, and can therefore be used to draw fine lines.

Eye level
Your eye level in relation to the subject that you are drawing can make a considerable difference to the composition and mood of the drawing. Viewing things from a high eye level (that it, looking down on them) separates elements in a scene from one another; when viewed from a low eye level (that is, looking up at them), elements tend to overlap.

Fixative
A substance sprayed on to drawings made in soft media such as charcoal, chalk and soft pastels to prevent them from smudging.

Foreshortening
The illusion that objects are compressed in length as they recede from your view.

Form
See **Modelling.**

Format
The shape of a drawing or painting. The most usual formats are landscape (a drawing that is wider than it is tall) and portrait (a drawing that is taller than it is wide), but panoramic (long and thin) and square formats are also common.

Graphite
Graphite is a naturally occurring form of crystallized carbon. To make a drawing tool, it is mixed with ground clay and a binder and then moulded or extruded into strips or sticks. The sticks are used as they are; the strips are

encased in wood to make graphite pencils. The proportion of clay in the mix determines how hard or soft the graphite stick or pencil is; the more clay, the harder it is.

Ground
A coating such as acrylic gesso or primer, which is applied to a drawing surface.

Hatching
Drawing a series of parallel lines, at any angle, to indicate shadow areas. You can make the shading appear more dense by making the lines thicker or closer together.

Crosshatching: a series of lines that crisscross each other at angles.

Highlight
The point on an object where light strikes a reflective surface. Highlights can be drawn by leaving areas of the paper white or by removing colour or tone with an eraser.

Line and wash
The technique of combining pen-and-ink work with a thin layer, or wash, of transparent paint (usually watercolour) or ink.

Manikin
A jointed wooden figure that can be moved into almost any pose, enabling the artist to study proportions and angles. Also known as a *lay figure*.

Mask
A material used to cover areas of a drawing, either to prevent marks from

touching the paper underneath or to allow the artist to work right up to the mask to create a crisp edge. There are three materials used for masking – masking tape, masking fluid and masking film (frisket paper). You can also simply cover up the relevant part of the drawing by placing a piece of paper over it.

Medium
The term has two very different meanings in art techniques:
1. The material in which an artist chooses to work – pencil, pen and ink, charcoal, soft pastel and so on. (The plural is 'media'.)
2. In painting, 'medium' is also a substance added to paint to alter the way in which it behaves – to make it thinner, for example. (The plural in this context is 'mediums'.)

Modelling
Emphasizing the light and shadow areas of a subject through the use of tone or colour, in order to create a three-dimensional impression.

Negative shapes
The spaces between objects in a drawing, often (but not always) the background to the subject.

Perspective
A system whereby artists can create the illusion of three-dimensional space on the two-dimensional surface of the paper.

Aerial perspective: the way the atmosphere, combined with distance, influences the appearance of things. Also known as *atmospheric perspective*.

Linear perspective: this system exploits the fact that objects appear to be smaller the further away they are from the viewer. The system is based on the fact that all parallel lines, when extended from a receding surface, meet at a point in space known as the vanishing point. When such lines are plotted accurately on the paper, the relative sizes of objects will appear correct in the drawing.

Single-point perspective: this occurs when objects are parallel to the picture plane. Lines parallel to the picture plane remain parallel, while parallel lines at 90˚ to the picture plane converge.

Two-point perspective: this must be used when you can see two sides of an object. Each side is at a different angle to the viewer and therefore each side has its own vanishing point. Parallel lines will slant at different angles on each side.

Picture plane
A imaginary vertical plane that defines the front of the picture area and corresponds with the surface of the drawing.

Positive shapes
The tangible features (figures, trees, buildings, still-life objects etc.) that are being drawn.

Recession
The effect of making objects appear to recede into the distance, achieved by using aerial perspective and tone. Distant objects appear paler in tone than those close by.

Sgraffito
The technique of scratching off pigment to reveal either an underlying colour or the white of the paper. The word comes from the Italian verb *graffiare*, which means 'to scratch'.

Sketch
A rough drawing or a preliminary attempt at working out a composition.

Support
The surface on which a drawing is made – usually paper, but board and surfaces prepared with acrylic gesso are also widely used.

Tint
A colour that has been lightened. In pure watercolour a colour is lightened by adding water to the paint.

Tone
The relative lightness or darkness of a colour.

Tooth
The texture of a support. Some papers are very smooth and have little tooth, while others – particularly those used for pastel drawings – have a very pronounced texture.

Torchon
A stump of tightly rolled paper with a pointed end, using for blending powdery mediums such as soft pastel, charcoal and graphite. Also known as paper stump or tortillon.

Vanishing point
In linear perspective, the vanishing point is the point on the horizon at which parallel lines appear to converge.

Viewpoint
The angle or position from which the artist chooses to draw his or her subject.

Warm colours
Colours in which yellow or red are dominant. They lie in the red-yellow half of the colour wheel and appear to advance.

Index